THE WAYWARD PIG AND OTHER FARM STORIES

SHANNA KELLEY

ISBN 978-1-64468-855-7 (Paperback)
ISBN 978-1-64468-856-4 (Digital)

Covenant Books, Inc.
11661 Hwy 707
Murrells Inlet, SC 29576
www.covenantbooks.com

In memory of Matthew Corley

To my husband, Ronnie. He has believed in me and has supported me with moving on and achieving my dreams. He is the rock in my corner, even when my ideas are crazy. He just goes along for the ride, no matter how bumpy it may get. Ronnie walks this path we call life right beside me through it all. He encourages me to reach my goals. I appreciate him more than he will ever know.

PROLOGUE

I started a blog a year ago and have now turned it into a book. There are several things I would like for you to know while reading this book.

The first thing is, I am a city girl. I always have been, so starting a farm and actually working this farm are an adventure all on its own. I was not ever into "getting my hands dirty" in a literal sense. I love animals and always have, but I was more of a dog and cat person. I did have the occasional rat or hermit crab in there somewhere. There were even a few snakes and some lizards at one point, but a farm? I just was not sure I could do it.

When my husband and I bought land, we had discussed having cattle and starting that kind of farm. I just thought Ronnie (my husband) would be doing that part of the farm. I had no desire to help with that. Could you see me standing in the middle of the road when a cow got out and yelling, "Here, cow, please come back?" I could see myself doing that, but that does not work. I also have a hard time with raising something that is going to be put on a table somewhere. I know that is what cattle is used for, but I did not think my heart could handle it. I was in for something that I was not prepared for with what happens next.

I would like to mention before we get into the fun reading, and it is quite funny reading about a city girl who turned farm girl and has no idea what she is doing, that life has not always been so good to me. I am a Christian, but years ago, I fell away from God, and it took me years to figure out why I was such a mess and faced so much trauma.

Right before this farm got started, I got a phone call from a lifelong friend. Her brother had committed suicide, and she needed me. I had grown up with both of them, and it shattered me, not like it did to her and her family, but it shattered me along with them. Regardless of blood, when you have been a part of someone's life that long, they are family. You never want to hear of something like this happening, but it is awful when it hits so close to home. He was so young and was such a great person when he was clean from drugs. He really battled a drug addiction for a long time. With drug addiction, there also comes depression. He battled that for a long time also. He lost his battle that day, and it was absolutely heartbreaking. He had so many people that loved him and would have helped him. They all tried so hard, but he gave up. I have known a lot of people my age and younger that have died early in life, but this one hit me really hard. I cannot understand it. His sister and I have been close for so long, but I watched him battle the drugs and the depression and the attempts to get clean, etc. That could be why this one hit me so hard. In this hitting me so hard, I realized I was not living the life I knew I was supposed to be living. I knew God was calling me to do something big and had been for years, but I continued to fight that. After this, I knew it was time to do what I was supposed to be doing.

When Matthew passed, I decided to do the things I loved and start the things I thought I would love. So I quit my job and started working for a nonprofit that was very dear to my heart. I got some animals on a farm to try to incorporate with my job, and I went back to school for a bachelor's degree in psychology. I had been talking about doing that for years, so now was a good time. I graduate this year.

It took a horrible tragedy to push me to do something different with my life. I decided to not wait for things anymore. I started this blog which is now turning into a book a month after we got our first animal. Some of this stuff will seem unbelievable, but I cannot make this stuff up. "The Lord is close to the brokenhearted and saves those who are crushed in spirit" (Psalm 34:18 NIV).

The one thing I want you to know the most is, these animals helped in healing some trauma and a hard heart. God has used all these animals and experiences to show me his love for me. I definitely had no idea what was going to come out of having this farm.

I hope you enjoy these stories. In looking back through some of them, they still make me laugh. Sometimes, I wonder, what was I thinking? Some of these things are just crazy, and going through it was even crazier.

Thank you for reading this book. I hope you enjoy it as much as I have writing it.

CHAPTER 1

Meet the First Farm Animal, Cracker Jack

He makes springs pour water into the ravines; it flows between the mountains. They give water to all the beasts of the field; the wild donkeys quench their thirst.
—Psalm 104:10–11

At the time of Ronnie and me talking about getting animals, something crazy happened. Maybe not crazy, more like, where did that come from? It really came out of nowhere and just landed in our lap.

I was doing home health physical therapy one day with a woman who lived not too far from me. Out of the blue, she said, "Do you want a donkey?" In my head, I was saying, "Why would I want a donkey?" My mouth actually said, "Well, I am not sure, let me talk to my husband." Turns out, the lady's daughter had the donkey and needed to rehome him.

I talked with Ronnie about the donkey. The donkey's name turned out to be Cracker Jack. He was a fourteen-year-old miniature donkey. I refused to look at him until Ronnie decided yes or no. Ronnie agreed to meet with the owner, and that did it. He agreed to take the donkey, Cracker Jack. What? We did not even have fencing up, food, water, supplies, or anything else needed. He made a deal with the owner for her to keep Cracker Jack a few more weeks so we could get everything set up for Cracker Jack.

Next thing I knew, I was outside helping build fencing, which I knew nothing about. It was quite the experience for me and for my poor husband trying to teach me to build fencing. What I did know that morning when we started to build fencing was it was twenty-five degrees and snowing in March. I definitely am not cut out for that, or so I thought. The fencing was not finished that day, but I did learn how to do it after a lot of trials and errors. I had no idea how hard it was to build fencing. I am not excited to have to do that again, but I am sure I will one day.

This is where it gets really good. Are you aware donkeys (well, most animals) are social animals? I did not know that. The reason Cracker Jack needed a new home was because his companion donkey, his mother, had passed away and he needed to be some where with other animals. Well, we only had some dogs and cats, so that would not work. What do we do now? I will get back to that question in a little bit.

So it is moving Cracker Jack day. Let's just say things did not go smoothly. My mom and dad came down to the house to help. My dad was helping with the fencing since I was not fast enough. After the fencing was finished, we borrowed a horse trailer, and the tires were flat, all of them. Ronnie had to fix that. Finally, we got over to get Cracker Jack, and the ground was too wet to pull the truck and trailer into the pasture where he was. I was hoping this was not a sign that this was a bad idea.

Cracker Jack is a smart but stubborn donkey. He did not want to go into the pasture to be able to get into the trailer. He was not going to do what was asked of him, but who could blame him? He did not know what was going on. He was going to fight us at every turn. The owner ended up putting a halter and lead rope on him. She did this after he tried to escape in the wrong direction three different times.

He got to the trailer after what seemed like hours. It was then learned he had never been in a trailer ever and he was fourteen years old. We tried treats, and that was a no. We tried the lead rope, and that was also a no. We tried pushing him, again a no. Ronnie, my dad, and the owner decided to just try to shut the door on him, nicely of course, and maybe he would go in. Yep, that one worked.

Poor Cracker Jack. He did not understand what was happening. He was a little scared with the transition but did well in the trailer. He jumped out quickly when we all got back to the house. I have never seen a three-hundred-pound animal be that quick. That could be because I have not been around too many of them in my life.

He ran around his new pen for a while. He ate some food and had some water. During all that, he was loved by his new family. He was sad and scared but did well his first night without his shelter built yet. My husband and I checked on him several times in the middle of the night, and he was pacing, but he was still fine.

In writing about this, I cannot imagine the emotions that donkey was feeling. I know he was scared, you could see that in his face. I can also bet he was a little heartbroken to not know what was happening and why he was leaving the only home he had known. Animals are smarter than we give them credit for, and this donkey had to be so confused.

The previous owner does still check on him to make sure he is okay. She has also been by to see him to make sure he was happy. She said she did not see him moping or pouting and was happy that he was happy. That meant a lot to me for her to see that. I promised her I would take good care of him, and that is what I am doing.

CHAPTER 2

The Friends

Two are better than one, because they have a good return for their labor; If either of them falls down, one can help the other up. But pity anyone who falls and has no one to help them up. Also, if two lie down together, they will keep warm. But how can one keep warm alone? Though one may be overpowered, two can defend themselves. A cord of three strands is not quickly broken.
                              —Ecclesiastes 4:9–12 (NIV)

It turns out, Cracker Jack was raised with goats. What is so convenient about that is Ronnie knew someone who would sale us some goats. That is a win-win situation right there. What was ever better is Ronnie arranged for us to go get the goats the day after we got Cracker Jack.

We showed up, and the family that had the goats started showing us around. Ronnie and I were walking into the pasture, and as the owner was calling for the goats, I saw two very small pink pigs running past me. I mentioned to Ronnie how cute they were, and he looked and me, and all he could say was no.

Now that was the first time my husband had ever told me no about anything. I took it as a challenge. That probably should not have been my attitude, but I am a work in progress. Back to the story, the lady overheard me talking about how cute the pigs were, and she said, "If you want them, you can have them." She said, "We are going to rehome them anyway, and one had already passed away."

At this point, I was determined to bring these pigs home. She said they were potbelly pigs, but I knew nothing about pigs, so they could have been farm pigs for all I knew. I had no idea and did not care in that moment. I was worried for their well-being. I mean, the owners were excellent caregivers to their animals, but she had said she did not know much about these pigs and was trying to learn more but had lost one of the sisters already.

My husband was just wanting to get the goats and go without the pigs. The goats are a dad and two of his male kids, which I learned, are called bucks. We got them up to where we were, and then the fun began, loading them. Two of them went into the trailer with no problems. The third one, on the other hand, well, no one knew that he did not like people at all. He ran all over the place. We all were trying to catch him. He finally got into the trailer, but it was a workout for all of us. I am sure he was scared and did not know what was going on which made things worse. The other two acted like it was no big deal.

Before we left, I asked my husband about the pigs again. I am all about rescuing strays and animals needing new homes. I actually do this with people too. My husband looked at me and said, "If you want them, you can have them but only if you can catch them." Now you have to remember, I know nothing about pigs. I learned really quickly how fast small pigs are. Luckily, the owner heard this and was able to lure them back into their pen and lock the gate so I could catch the pigs. She, the owner, actually caught one, and I caught the other one. Even in a locked pen, they were fast and very hard to catch. I was laughing so hard trying to run and catch them that I am sure I was putting on quite the show. I knew my husband was laughing at me because I could hear him. I still laugh thinking about that.

The next thing I learned quickly was, pigs scream when they are picked up. They have a high-pitched squeal that will make your ears ring. They hated me already, and they were not even home yet. What was I thinking? Maybe this was a bad idea. We were about to find out.

Ronnie got all the animals situated, and we started out on the hour and a half drive home. When we got there, I realized I was going to have to catch those pigs again out of the trailer before we could get the goats out. I was not sure if I was up for catching them again, but it had to be done.

Let me say this after over an hour-long drive, I now had new obstacles. Those obstacles would be urine and feces from goats and pigs. So while chasing pigs, one at a time, I was now slipping and sliding in a trailer. After about thirty minutes or so, I had both of them out of the trailer and in the old kennel at the back of our property with some straw and some water. I still did not know what to feed them, so I thought we had some vegetables or something like that for them.

At this time, the goats—which we named Hercules, Lucky, and Romeo, we also have Cracker Jack—they were meeting for the first time. It was an instant connection. Cracker Jack kind of lit up and was so happy to have some friends. I was so glad to see this. He had been lonely for so long. It truly was an indescribable moment. I saw the light in his eyes come back. I have never experienced anything like that.

Now my poor husband and I could still say this today, he was really put to work when we got these animals. Now fifteen minutes after we got home, it started raining. Oh no. We did not have the shelter built yet. So my husband put one up, not completely finished, but something up to get them out of the rain. He is a wonderful man and usually goes along with my crazy schemes. I was so grateful for him for building that in the rain. I am still grateful for all he does for me and these animals. Wow, what a day it was.

CHAPTER 3

Sickness

*Nevertheless, I will bring health and healing to it; I will heal my
people and will let them enjoy abundant peace and security.*
—Jeremiah 33:6 (NIV)

This is where the story starts to get wild and why I have learned to
love pigs during this farm transition in my life. I noticed the night
we brought the animals home that one of the pigs, the smaller one,
did not look right. Now remember, I knew nothing about pigs at all

when we picked them up, but I knew something was wrong. I felt it in my gut.

I spent way too much time with the pigs even from day one. They were in a small space in a kennel so I could get to know them and try to socialize them to get used to me. They would hide in the straw and were not friendly at all. They would scream when I would go into the pen. They were so scared. Seeing them so small and so scared really did break my heart for them.

My routine was to go out and feed everyone in the mornings and spend more time with all them in the evening after feeding and watering. It really was work, more than I had envisioned. What did I know about a farm anyway? Because I was spending so much time with them and this was just the first week, I noticed how bad one of the pig's skin was, I mean almost turning black and her breathing was horrendous. What was happening? What was this? What was I supposed to do now?

I was home alone, my husband was out of town, so I started calling people I knew to see what they thought. These were people who had a pig or had had a pig so not random people. One of them said she looked dirty and to try to give her a bath. I could not bring her in the house, so even in the colder weather, I gave the pig a bath outside with a water hose, soap, and scrub brush.

I would never know how the cops did not show up at my house with all that screaming. It sounded like someone was getting hurt. After I gave her a bath and scrubbed off some of the black skin, I wrapped her in a towel, and she relaxed enough to let me hold her to keep her warm. Her breathing was starting to get worse. She was now wheezing, loudly. I recorded it and sent it to my friends, and both said it was pneumonia and to get her to a vet now. I called the emergency vet, but they did not see pigs. It was Sunday night, so I knew I would have to get this pig to the vet in the morning.

What I did not know was because pigs are a prey animal, they do not show signs of sickness until it is almost too late. I worried all night long about this pig who we had named Treat. That was my husband's idea. The other one became Spam. I would also mention that after I put her back in the kennel with Spam and went in the house, I noticed I had started to break out in a rash. I was wondering if I was allergic. That would have been horrible if I was allergic to my new pigs.

The next morning, Treat was still alive. I rushed her to the vet in town in a cat carrier since she was so small. Treat was in bad shape. I was starting to panic. My rash had also spread, and I was in bad shape. We were both miserable. The vet asked me what I thought was wrong with her, and I told him I thought she had pneumonia, so he gave me an antibiotic to give her. He never took her out of the crate. I asked about her skin, and he said he did not know what it was. What? Well, neither did I, but it was not good.

I got her home and attempted to wrap a pill in a tortilla with peanut butter. If you have never been around a pig, they are extremely smart, which I still was not aware of. She spat that thing out so fast. I found it and just tried to give it to her. Well, I got bit, not badly bit but bit, anyway. So I finally just shoved it down her throat and prayed I still had my hand after it was over. I got it down her that way.

A few days passed, and she was not any better, and neither was my rash. Oh, the joys, what have I done. Why did I not just listen to my husband? I really could not give up. I just had to keep trying even though it was not looking good. I might lose her. Even so, I owed it to her and Spam to do everything possible to save her.

I called another vet, where we took our dogs, and asked if there was a vet there that would see pigs. Yes, they did and had an appointment for the next day. I took her in, and he said she did have pneumonia but she also had sarcoptic mange. He looked at me and asked if I had a rash yet. Well, yes, I did. It was horrible. If I was that bad, I could only imagine how bad the pig felt. The vet told me what to do for myself and for her. My husband gave her antibiotic injections for the next three days for the pneumonia.

Spam ended up with the sarcoptic mange also, so I was glad I had enough stuff to get rid of that from her also. I was so glad they were in a small space to be able to spray them; they hated that and hated me for it. The socializing of these pigs definitely took several steps back after that.

I prayed so hard for Treat to live. To some, that would seem silly, but for me, I was able to see God's answer to my prayers. He was still with me and still cared for me. He answered my prayers. My girl, Treat, lived and was starting to thrive.

CHAPTER 4

The Wayward Pig

My brothers and sisters, if one of you should wander from the truth and someone should bring that person back, remember this: Whoever turns a sinner from the error of their way will save them from death and cover over a multitude of sins.
—James 5:19–20 (NIV)

Now you get to see why I named this the wayward pig. The pigs were growing so much, and they were still in that little kennel. I was trying to get the pens outside ready. Ronnie and I were spraying the weeds and checking fencing to make sure it would keep them in. It was a slow process.

One night, I went in their little kennel to feed them. I turned around and bumped the gate. I turned back around, and Treat was gone. I mean, gone. I took off after her, running. Keep in mind, I am new at this and not in the best shape. Now picture this: the kennel was at the very back of the property beside a creek, woods, briars, and honeysuckle, and now I had a pig loose in all that. I put all fears of what was in the woods away and started running. I did remember to shut the gate to keep Spam in.

I was running through the woods with muck boots on, capri pants, and a T-shirt on. I was getting cut up and eaten by mosquitoes. Treat did not care, she was free. Daisy, my lab, was running after her also. Remember, pigs are scary smart and survivors by instinct. She did not want to come back. She ended up in the creek. Ummm, I know there were snakes in there, I was from the city, but she was my baby. I ran through the creek. She started back up the embankment, and Daisy scared her enough she had to stop to use the bathroom. I was able to catch her at that point.

I realized after this that yet again, my prayers were being answered. I was so mad at Treat, but she was feeling better and wanted out. I cannot say I blamed her, she and Spam were in a tight space. I was also truly grateful she was over her sickness. I got her back, though, that was the important part of this.

CHAPTER 5

It Happened Again

*I will seek that which was lost and bring again that which
was driven away, and will bind up that which was broken,
and will strengthen that which was sick: but I will destroy
the fat and the strong; I will feed them with judgement.*
— Ezekiel 34:16 (KJV)

A month later, I was really feeling bad about the cramped living the pigs were in. I had joined several pages on social media to learn all I could about pigs and had seen people walk pigs with a harness and a leash. I talked my husband into going to get a couple for me to try it. Looking back, I am not sure what I was thinking since they still were not socialized and still hated me.

He went to the store and brought a couple home. He bought small harnesses since he really had not seen how much they had grown in the short amount of time. He was amazed. I tried the small, it did not work. He went back and got medium harnesses, but that would not work either. They were so mad at me after all that.

I went back in later, and again, I bumped the gate and out went Treat. It was like she was just waiting for me to do that again so she could escape. Spam was throwing the biggest fit I had ever seen. I was chasing her, Ronnie was chasing her, and Daisy was chasing her. This time, it went on for hours, and it was turning dark. We finally gave to give up and leave her out there.

I was in distress and crying my eyes out. We lived where there were tons of coyotes, bears, and I was almost certain I had seen a cougar. I was being negative and thinking, *This is it, she will not survive this now. She is out and alone in the dark with predators.*

I went to work the next day, and I was so depressed and upset. My husband searched for hours for her. He was cut up form the briars and said he had seen a lot of snakes but no sign of her. I was not ready to give up on her. I continued to search with no luck. I did not even see a sign of her. She was just gone. Spam was so depressed and would not eat. It was so awful.

That day passed, and I was thinking she was not coming back. In my head, I knew an animal had gotten to her. I went to check on Spam when I got home, and there was Treat, asleep next to the kennel where Spam was. It scared me because I was not expecting that. When I became startled, she ran off again. I did not chase her this time, but my hope had returned. If she came back once, she would do it again.

When I got home the next day, my husband had left for work again, so I was on my own. I put my boots on before I let the dogs out so I could hopefully catch her if she was still there. Again, I was not fast enough. These little potbelly pigs are super smart and superfast.

I let the dogs out and had Daisy help me chase her. She was all over the place. She passed the property line where there was barbed wire fence and sat down. Daisy was with her at this point. She sat right passed the barbed wire fence knowing I could not get to her. She let me pet her but would not budge from that spot.

I went back to check on Spam. This was so rough on her. She was a mess, but in that minute, she was calm. I did not understand how she was so calm because she had been throwing a fit. Then I heard it, oinking, right next to me. Somehow, this pig had beaten me back out of the woods and was hiding in the straw in the kennel. The way she was positioned, she could not run away again, so I was able to grab her and get her back in the pen. She was tired, hungry, and thirsty. She was home, and I was happy. Spam was mad at her, but she was happy too.

CHAPTER 6

Lost a Third Time

What do you think? If a man owns a hundred sheep, and one of them wanders away, will he not leave the ninety-nine on the hills and go to look for the one that wandered off? And if he finds it, truly I tell you, he is happier about that one sheep than about the ninety-nine that did not wander off. In the same way your Father in heaven is not willing that any of these little ones should perish.
—Matthew 18:12–14 (NIV)

A few days later, I ordered harnesses that would fit the pigs. Apparently, I do not learn lessons quickly. I attempted to use the harnesses. What happened? You guessed it: I bumped the gate, and Treat was gone again, and Spam was throwing a fit. Do you see a pattern? Treat is the wayward pig, and Spam is the good girl that does not leave home.

I had to stop and laugh about it at this point. This was really my fault and not the pig's fault. This was the third time in a month, and I had not learned what I should have after the first two times. Will I ever learn? Probably not.

This time, I did not chase her. I did not call Daisy to chase her. Daisy had become my pig chaser, and she loved it. She never hurt Treat in any way, but she remained with her during her escapes from her small prison.

What I realized with this third escape was she never really went anywhere. She stayed close to home to stay by Spam. I think they were planning to break her out also and run away. After a few minutes, here came Treat, coming back and oinking up a storm at Spam. She saw that I was still there in the kennel and ran off again.

This time was different from the other two times. Spam was literally throwing herself at the chain-link fence until her nose was bleeding. Treat was staying where I could see her, but she would not let me close to her. I sat in the kennel and tried to calm Spam, but who was I kidding? She hated me still. I sat there so long, I could hear Treat trying to communicate with Spam, and then I heard Spam communicating with Spam. It would be hilarious if it was not such a bad situation.

Apparently, pigs love a good game of hide-and-seek. Treat and I did this for not hours, this time, it was days. She would run, and I would hide, and then she would see me and run and hide for days. It was so frustrating. I knew she was not far away because I would have my dog, Daisy, go find her. Treat would oink, and I would know she was okay.

I started praying again that I would catch this pig. I did not want anything bad to happen to her. I needed her to come home and be back in the kennel, not only for me but also for Spam who was yet again very depressed and upset. I prayed I would not lose either of them through all this.

The third night of this, I decided to leave food and water out for Treat. I knew she had to be hungry. When I came out the next morning, the food was still there. I immediately panicked and thought the worst. Nope, she was in the kennel, talking to Spam. I knew my prayer again had been answered. I knew this because pigs have excellent hearing since they have such poor eyesight. She did not even turn in my direction, and I was able to grab her. I startled her, and she, of course, started screaming, but I got her back in that kennel. Spam was so mad at her she would not let her eat. Treat was so exhausted she just went to sleep. She slept mostly for several days after this last escape. I did not care, she was safe. I knew that that new pen needed to be finished.

CHAPTER 7

More?

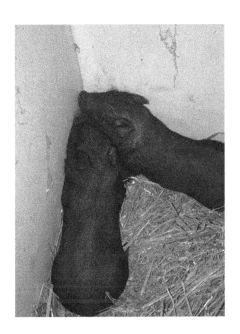

And God is able to bless you abundantly, so that in all things at all times, having all that you need, you will abound in every good work.
—2 Corinthians 9:8 (NIV)

During the second escape when Treat ran away, I reached out to some people about getting another pig for Spam to have a companion in case Treat did not come back. I really was not sure if Treat was coming back or if she was not coming back. I did not want Spam to be lonely. Not really sure what I was thinking, Spam was a mean and aggressive pig. No lie, she would lunge at me and try to bite me when I went into the kennel. I was not scared, though, since I had learned her movements.

I had scheduled to pick up a piglet and then cancelled it when Treat came back. Then I reached out again when Treat ran off the third time and decided to not cancel it. What was I thinking? I still do not know.

I went by the farm where the pigs for sale were. He had two piglets left, and they were so small and so terrified. They were a brother and sister. I could not take one without the other because of their bond. I just could not do it. They were so scared.

I was going to say, before I finish this story, there is a huge pig problem in the United States. At the point I got these two pigs, I had no idea there was a pig population problem. I still did not know much about pigs. After learning more, I would not get any pig from a breeder again. I will talk more about this later in the book.

The two new pigs were named Pork Chop and Bacon Bit. They were so cute. They were not socialized either. So I had four pigs now that were not socialized. I was definitely in for more work that I had planned.

Pork Chop and Bacon Bit were stuck together like glue. They were still terrified of everything. The two of them were eating, drinking, and sleeping well in the kennel a few doors down from Spam and Treat. They all would oink at each other often. It was so cute to sit and listen to.

One thing I did with Pork Chop and Bacon Bit with trying to socialize them was to pick them up and hold them until they would stop screaming. In my head, I thought it would help them to get used to me. That definitely did not happen. It made things much worse.

CHAPTER 8

Farm Things Learned

Be sure you know the condition of your flocks,
give careful attention to your herds.
— Proverbs 27:23 (NIV)

By now, Ronnie and I had been handling the farm for three months. So much had happened in those three short months. This city girl was learning a lot on the farm. I want to tell you a few of these things.

Donkeys are known for being stubborn. This donkey was no different. Cracker Jack would bray in the mornings starting around five o'clock in the morning until he got fed. He loved his hay, and he would fight the goats to get to the hay. He and the goats had become the best of friends. Cracker Jack and Lucky had quite the bond. The last thing about Cracker Jack was he was fiercely protective of all three of the goats.

Hercules, the biggest goat and the dad of Romeo and Lucky, was demanding in getting attention. He wanted all the attention. He would headbutt me when I come through the gate. He would bite off the buttons on my clothes and untie shoes. He had a big personality.

Romeo, oh, Romeo. I named him correctly. He wanted to be loved on. He would sit in my lap. He would sit and let me pet him as long as I could. He even would lick the side of my face. He was the sweetest animal we had.

Lucky was not friendly. He was so scared of humans. He was a nice little goat, but he was so skittish. Not sure what happened to him, and the owners did not know either. He loved to run around, and he acted so happy, he was just very leery of humans. That too was still a work in progress.

I had learned that farming was very hard work. It did not matter what the weather was, the animals had to have food and fresh water. They all deserved to have the best care. They would love you unconditionally.

I had learned that I could do more on the farm that I originally thought. I was hauling buckets of water, and I was getting up early to feed, and having animals was a healing thing mentally. My nails were always dirty now, I usually had straw in my hair, and I was finding muscles I had forgotten I had. This was work, but it was rewarding for me anyway. It was healing for me and for the animals.

CHAPTER 9

Tornado

When calamity overtakes you like a storm, when disaster sweeps over you like a whirlwind, when distress and trouble overwhelm you.
—Proverbs 1:27 (NIV)

I am going to add to the crazy story. The weekend Pork Chop and Bacon Bit got here, the weather got wild here in Arkansas. That is normal, though. You never know what it is going to do around here. To top everything off, my husband was not home.

It was a Saturday afternoon. I had been outside with all the animals, giving food, water, and attention. The sky started turning dark, so I went inside to work on some homework, I was still working on my bachelors of psychology degree. I am not one that scares easily over the weather. I did not turn on the news or any of that. It is Arkansas; it could change at any moment. I went inside, and the electricity went out.

Next thing I knew, I had fallen asleep and was waking up after three hours. The electricity was still out, and the weather was so much worse. The rain was pouring like crazy, and the wind was wild. I jumped off the couch and ran outside to check all the animals. The donkey and goats were in their shelter and seemed to be okay. I ran down to the kennels to check on the pigs, and they were all warm and dry also.

I went back inside but just had some weird feeling in my gut. My phone was almost dead, so I went outside to my car to charge it just in case. I continued to run back and forth between pens and the house to make sure all the animals were okay. (I also had three dogs and two cats in the house, some of them do not like storms.) In reality, I was starting to get nervous.

I went back outside, and the rain had not stopped, and the wind continued to pick up speed. I was officially nervous, not for me but for my animals. I got down on my hands and knees in the mud while it was raining and prayed for protection around the house and all the animals. I wanted to make sure that they were going to be fine.

I finally went back inside to the electricity coming back on after six hours. My husband and family had called because apparently as I was outside running around, there was a tornado that had gone through close to our house. We do not hear the tornado sirens out here where we live, and I do not watch the news, so I had no clue that this was happening so close to the house. My focus was on keeping the animals safe. I did not realize until two days later that the tornado had touched down less than half a mile up the road for me. God really had my back on that one. All I could say was, "Thank you, Jesus."

CHAPTER 10

Another One?

For every kind of beast and bird, of reptile and sea creature,
can be tamed and has been tamed by mankind.
—James 3:7 (ESV)

The same weekend of the storm, I was looking through social media. I was on several pig sites to learn more about pigs. I really knew nothing about pigs, and I had four to care for. I wanted to give them the best life possible. I saw a post about a pig needing a home. This is also before I learned about the pig population, but I am getting there in the story. I did not think much about the pig until five different people messaged me about this particular pig. I even had a girl call me about this pig. What was I supposed to do?

I told my friend to give the lady my phone number, and I would see what was happening. The lady texted me and gave me the story. My head was saying, *Do not do it*, but my heart was saying, *Do it*. I told her she would have to wait a few weeks if I took the pig because I needed to get some pens built for them. She said that was fine.

How do I tell my husband we were about to have five pigs? I do not think he really even liked the pigs much at this point. He was not going to be happy about this. Would the pigs even get along? How would this work? Would there be a pen built soon enough? I was becoming a crazy pig lady.

The pen finally was built. The hog panels were up already. Ronnie built them a lean to and put railroad ties around everything so that Treat and Spam could not get out. I was so excited that they finally had some room to run around.

It was time to move Treat and Spam to the outside pen. I knew I could not do it alone, so I asked my husband to help me. These pigs were still not friendly, and they were hard to catch if they decided to run, which you have seen in this book. I got Treat out first because she was smaller and less aggressive. She screamed so loud, I thought I still have some hearing loss. I got her in the pen, and she started running around. I saw her wagging her tail for the first time since her last prison break.

Now came Spam. She fought me really hard. She was running in circles and would not let me grab her. I finally got her, and she started thrashing around and screaming like a child throwing a tantrum. My husband had been standing at the gate laughing at me (do you see a pattern with me chasing pigs, that is how this whole thing started), he opened it and went to open the other gate for me. What he did not realize was he had just trapped me in the kennel. I had to get that gate shut to get out of the kennel. I finally got this down while Spam was still thrashing and screaming. I walked as fast as I could to get her in the pen. I almost dropped her as I was going up the hill. I finally got her in the pen.

I was not exaggerating when I told you there was an instant attitude adjustment for both Treat and Spam. They had so much more room, and they were completely healthy and ready for it. They could run and play. They were wagging tails, almost as a thank-you. Them being that happy made me so happy for them.

The conversation about the fifth pig finally came up. I told him the story about the pig and its silence, cricket silence. I continued to talk, and there continued to be silence. At this point, I was seeing his side to this conversation without him talking. It went something like this with no words. "We have four already. We also have a donkey, three goats, two cats, and three dogs. You drive an hour to work and back every day, and you are in school. Why do you think you need another pig?" Did he say this? No, but I felt it. And he was right. He finally asked who had the pig. I did not understand why that mattered in the moment, but I told him. What came next, I did not expect. He then told me he knew her and she was actually family, "So take the pig." But if it was anyone else, we would not be doing it. So here came another pig. Gus was coming here for his new home.

CHAPTER 11

Happy Goats and Donkey

*Who teaches us more than the beasts of the earth and
makes us wiser than the birds of the heavens?*
—Job 35:11 (ESV)

I know I am talking about the pigs a lot, but that is in the name of
the book. I am going to tell you some things I have learned about
goats during this farm life. I am from the city and did not know any
of these things before having them. I am a learn-as-you-go girl with
this farm.

Goats get something in their stomachs if they eat too much of the wrong food called bloat. It is a painful condition for the goat. They need medicine when they get bloat. I have not had to deal with this yet, but I have been doing research. At one point, I thought Romeo had it because his stomach was do distended, but he was not in any visible pain and continued to eat and drink without at problem.

Hercules had started losing his hair horribly. He looked really mangey. I was not sure what was going on. I researched it and turned out if a goat had a mineral deficiency, they would lose their hair. I got a new mineral block for them, and his hair came back.

This was something I had no idea would happen and was a little gross. Goats, during mating season, will actually urinate in their beards to become more attractive. Hercules and Romeo both do this, and then they try to rub it on me. Sorry, not happening, get away from me with all that. Lucky does this also, but he still is not sure about me and keeps his distance.

Cracker Jack was food aggressive. He would run all the goats off from the food bowls to be able to eat what he wanted. He would also kick at them and bray at them until they leave at least one food bowl. He was really rude about it. He had not hurt any of the goats; they knew to move out of the way.

I have also learned that the goats love to eat leaves off a tree more than they like the grass. Ronnie had said that, and then my dad showed us that. There was a tree in their pen, and he went out and pulled down some limbs for them to eat off, and they devoured it in minutes. I had started doing this for them also. They loved it. It was cute until they jumped up on me like a dog; those hooves were brutal when they hit you.

When either my husband or I came outside, the goats and Cracker Jack all ran to the fence. They loved the attention. Cracker Jack would run into me and almost knock me over when going into the pen. Hercules and Romeo would headbutt each other over attention. They all fought over attention, except Lucky, and he still was not sure what was happening. He was always happy to see us, as long as we were on the other side of the fence.

Lucky and Cracker Jack have become bonded and go everywhere together, so I am not too worried about Lucky. I think he will come around at some point. Part of the issue could have been my husband tackling Lucky so I could pet him one night. I think that caused a bit of a regression with Lucky liking humans.

Romeo would sit in my lap, he would bite me on the face, he would pose for selfies with me. He would also try to eat my clothes and would jump on me like a dog. Hercules would try to eat my clothes, and he tried to bite my fingers. It was really an odd thing to me. I had never been around goats, so I did not know what to expect. It was definitely an experience.

CHAPTER 12

Here's Gus

*But ask the animals, and they will teach you, or the birds in the
sky, and they will tell you; or speak to the earth, and it will teach
you, or let the fish in the sea inform you. Which of all these does
not know that the hand of the Lord has done this? In his hand
is the life of every creature and the breath of all mankind.*
—Job 12:7–10

It was time to pick up Gus. I got all the details and decided to get him on my way home from work on day. I was not prepared for what took place on this adventure. Gus was an inside pig and well trained, so I did not have a care in the world. I just know this was going to go smoothly.

I got to the meeting spot, and the lady I was getting him from pulled in night after me. Gus was in her lap. He liked car rides on someone's lap. We talked for a while, and she put him in my lap for the drive home. He was a little bigger than my other pigs, and he did not know me. What could go wrong? He started to throw a fit, and she gave him treats. We decided to say goodbye so I could get Gus home and settled.

Here is where the funny parts begin. Picture this: a potbelly pig on my lap. They were not usually friendly with people they did not know well. He was just handed over to someone he did not know and was sitting on my lap. He had no idea what was going on or where he was going.

We lived about thirty minutes from where I picked Gus up. I was not expecting this ride home. He started to panic in my lap. He was throwing a fit, but I had nowhere to pull over. I was trying to hold him in one place with one arm and use my other hand to drive. The car started to move off the road because he was so big and was getting under the steering wheel while I was trying to drive. I got my seat back some and got back on the road correctly. I was not five minutes into the trip.

The next ten minutes, he was fighting me so much. I was still trying to hold him and drive. Next thing I knew, my rear window was going down because he was standing on the button. I got that back up after a minute or two. He was trying to get away from me, and I was fighting to hold him; he kicked my car into neutral. Oh my, this was a rough ride. I got it back into drive and carried on down the road. Only ten more minutes to go, would we make it? I was not sure at this point.

We had been driving twenty minutes. He had been fighting me for fifteen of those minutes. I was exhausted, and he was getting there. He started to relax, but what did pigs do when they were scared? They use the bathroom. I thought that we were almost home, and I felt something wet in my lap. This was not a little wet, this was wet all the way down my legs and up to my back. Then he started to poop in the car, on my lap. There was nothing I could do but laugh. I laughed at this. I never would have done that a few months ago. Poor Gus was nervous. I could not be mad at him.

I got him home and carried him down to the pen with Treat and Spam. He screamed at me, but I needed a shower and cleaned my car out. I did both of these things and then went to watch the introduction to the other pigs. I had never seen one before but had read research saying it could really look brutal between the pigs.

There was quite a bit of circling each other there for a while in the pen. Spam and Treat did not know what to think. There was now a boy in their pen. Thankfully, he was already neutered. When the food came out, that was when things changed. Treat and Spam had always shared a bowl, but now Gus was there. I learned quickly that one bowl would not be enough. The fighting broke out, and just like I had heard, it was brutal. I had also heard if you put Vaseline on the pig's ears and body, the other pig's teeth would just roll off the body so it would not cut through the skin. I ran to get the Vaseline. I only put it on Gus, though, because the other two pigs still were not friendly too much with me and Gus was so scared, he was not fighting back.

I did not want to do this, but I walked away from the fighting. They needed to work out who would be top hog. In my research, I read if you break up the fighting, it goes on longer. I went to bed very unsettled. I did not want any of them to be hurt. I prayed most of the night and did not sleep much.

I got up the next morning, and they were all alive. Gus was not sleeping in the lean to, he was outside of it on his blanket, but they were all alive. It looked like there were some cuts but nothing terrible. Gus must have started fighting back since they all had cuts on them. In a weird sense, I was grateful for that. I needed to go to work and debated on taking Gus with me, but I knew they still had to work it out. I went to work still nervous.

By the time I got home and I raced home as fast as I could, they were all in the lean together. Treat and Spam were definitely all cut up. It looked like Gus made top hog after all. He beat up on those ladies for sure. They worked it out, and in twenty-four hours, they were all friends. There again, God answered my prayers.

Oh, Gus. He was the fifth pig on this farm. All four of the other pigs on the farm, I was still working with to socialize. Gus was already socialized. He would cuddle, loved to be petted, run to the gate ready to get loved on, and give kisses. He was the absolute sweetest pig.

CHAPTER 13

For the Son of Man came to seek and to save the lost.
—Luke 19:10 (NIV)

I have mentioned Daisy a few times in some of these stories. It is probably because she is in everything that happens on this farm. She has turned out to be an excellent farm dog, better than ever expected. Daisy is also a rescue. Her story is not something that happens every day.

My brother-in-law, Tyler, had been working on a side by side here at the house. It was before the farm started. He left to go get some parts for the side by side. Ronnie and I were outside doing yard work that day. Tyler came back from the store with a dog. I jumped off the lawn mower to see what in the world was going on.

We had lost a dog in death, a few months earlier, I was not ready to add another dog to our two old dogs. I think Tyler saw the look on my face. He decided to let me know he could not leave the dog where he found her and he would be taking her home to find her another home. I was not really upset about any of this.

By this point, I was on the ground with this beautiful lab mix puppy. She was a gorgeous puppy. She had a shiny coat of fur and looked well cared for. She did not look like the normal stray you find. Here is how the story went. There were a couple kids in the parking lot with the dog that had been taking care of her, but the landlord would not let them keep her, so she needed a home. According to Tyler, the dog followed him into the store, so he put her in a cart throughout the store and decided to bring her home. Of course, the story melted my heart. It did not help that she was so sweet and was loving the attention she was getting. Do you see where this is going?

The next thing I knew, my husband came around the corner and saw this dog who could not have been more than three months old. He bent down and said, "Daisy, come here, Daisy." This dog took off in a running sprint toward him like she had known him her whole life. It was like a scene out of the movie *Annie*. It was so sweet. Daisy received a name and a home that day because she was in the right place at the right time. She had been the best farm dog. She truly was an asset to the farm and the occasional pain because she loved to roam around, but I was glad she was here. She was not my dog. She was definitely Ronnie's dog. There was no question about that.

She loved the water, loved to roam the farm, loved to just be a dog. This girl was a mess. She also protected the house. She stayed outside quite a bit, but she was an inside dog also. When it was dark out and she was still out, she walked the yard and barked if there was anything out there. The one thing she did do that I could not stand was she hunted the area for critters. She brought me chickens, rabbits, moles, bones, and possums. She was a good hunter, but I usually either had to save the animal or I had to dispose of the animal. I do not care for that part, but I do love this dog.

CHAPTER 14

The Other Animals

*My people have been lost sheep, their shepherds have led them
astray and caused them to roam on the mountains. They wondered
over mountain and hill and forgot their own resting place.*
—Jeremiah 50:6 (NIV)

Ronnie and I already had two dogs and two cats—Maggie, Pepper,
Bubba, and Persia—before we moved out with some land. These

guys were here before Daisy came to the farm. They were my animals when Ronnie and I got married. I have had them for ten years now. I always lived in the city with a fenced yard, so when we moved out here, there was no fence. They did not know the boundaries of this yard. What happens? They run off, out of the yard. We had a pit bull, Beaux, at the time of moving; he has passed away now, though. Anyway, they all ran off. Ronnie got in the truck to go find them. He found Pepper and Beaux quickly but not Maggie. Maggie was gone. It took two days to find her. Luckily, we had already met one of the neighbors, and he spotted her about a mile up the road from the house, so Ronnie went to look for her and was able to bring her home. She was hungry, thirsty, and exhausted.

Not long after this, Maggie started having seizures and needed medicine with a possible brain tumor. That was a struggle for a while. She was still happy and still running off but close to the house now. Pepper had arthritis and struggled to walk some days, but she had not left the yard since then.

Getting Persia and Bubba was an experience for sure. Persia and Bubba both have interesting stories. Persia was astray I found in the backyard starving and had a belly full of worms and infested with fleas. I did not want a cat, but I fell in love with her. She came into the house and got a bath and a vet appointment. She was still my sweet girl. Bubba was astray found in a car engine with his lip cut halfway off. He was taken to the emergency vet and fixed up. I knew someone there, and the cat needed a home. Persia needed a friend, so he came to live with me.

Bubba and Persia are also ten years old. There are so many stories I could tell you about these two. I will tell you a story on each of them since we have moved to the country. The first one is about Persia. She is a sneaky thing when she wants to be. One night, someone left the back door opened from the kitchen. Persia loved to sneak out of the house at the old house, so an opened door with no one watching was like a dream come true for her. It had been a couple of hours since I had seen her but did not think too much about it because the house was so much bigger than our old one. I went around the corner after hours had passed by and saw the door was cracked. We now lived on acreage with wild animals present and my cat was missing. This was not good for my soul.

I started yelling for her, and my husband came to the kitchen asking what was wrong, so I told him what had happened. He said something like, "I bet I left the door opened since I did go out there, so I am going to go ahead and go pack my bags since she is now missing." I laughed because that was ridiculous, or was it? *Wink, wink.* Anyway, we called her name and nothing. By now, it was pitch-black outside. Of course, my heart had dropped into my stomach, and I thought the worst. I walked away for a bit to calm my nerves and prayed. When I came back around the corner, she was standing at the door looking in. Her eyes were saying, I am finished out here now, so can you let me back in now. I scooped her up and cried and cuddled her. She had never tried to run away again.

On to Bubba and his story. Bubba has never been a very friendly cat. He will sit in your lap and want to be petted, and when he gets tired of it, he will bite you and move on. After we got the other animals, he changed all that. He started to become more affectionate. He wanted attention all the time.

The night, I came in from giving Treat a bath outside, I was soaked, so I took off my clothes and set them in the floor so I could get a shower. My plan was to put them in the washing machine right after I got out of the shower. I got out of the shower and saw Bubba peeing on my clothes. He had never done that before, ever. He was litter boxed trained and had never had an accident anywhere. I could not believe what I was seeing. I scolded him a bit, and he ran off. I thought he was jealous. I take that back, I do not think, I know he was. He did this a few more times, and then I guess he decided it was not working and he stopped. He has continued to be very loving and affectionate through since getting all the animals. That has not changed. I do work harder at making sure he does not feel so neglected so he does not feel the need to pee on my clothing anymore, though.

Pepper is my baby. She was the first animal I got in this group. When she was about three months old, she fell off the deck and broke her back leg. She had to be in a splint for a long time. Poor little girl. She got lots of cuddling and lots of love during this time. She became very spoiled during that time. She has never been an active dog because of that. Now that we live on the farm, this dog has opened up and become a different dog. She is running and playing and acting like she is a puppy again. She is the momma dog of all the others. She actually tells on them, and she scolds them. It is so funny to watch.

CHAPTER 15

The Dreaded Harness

Forget the former things; do not dwell on the past. See, I am doing
a new thing! Now it springs up; do you not perceive it? I am
making a way in the wilderness and streams in the wasteland.
—Isaiah 43:18–19 (NIV)

I am sure you remember the tragic attempts at using a harness with these pigs. I decided to go ahead and try with Gus since he was already a socialized pig. It took me several times to get the harness on him, but I was able to get it on him. I then tried to get him to walk with the harness. That was a big no. He threw a giant fit. I let go of the leash, and he ran around the pen for a bit. He calmed down, and I tried again. This attempt was also a big no. I decided he was under too much stress, so I stopped. I sat down and petted him and told him what a good boy he was for trying. He rolled over and stayed there for belly rubs. Of course, Spam and Treat had to go check on him and smell the harness. I am sure they were remembering the trauma they had been through with the harness.

A few weeks later, it was time to try again with the harness. This time, I had family over to watch the show. My stepdaughter, Jodie; her boyfriend, Braiden; my parents; and my husband were all at the house for this. Jodie and Braiden got in the pen with Gus, Treat, and Spam. Gus is the only friendly one and loved attention, so they were loving on him. I decided to try the harness while they were there to help me.

I got the harness on him and started making a line of Cheerios on for him. This worked. He started walking on the leash out of the pen. This was success for me and for Gus. I was so excited. I got excited too soon. Gus got agitated because he was too far from Treat and Spam. He had no problem running back to the pen to be with the girls. He was definitely already bonded to the girls. It really made me happy to see this.

This has become one of his favorite things to do. He throws a huge fit when he has to go back in the pen, but he does not leave Treat and Spam for long still. He will now even come out of the pen without a leash. He does not leave the area at all. He is such a good pig. He has no problem with putting the leash on him. There is no fit throwing with him getting the harness on. It is really funny how things change so much. He is used to it now.

CHAPTER 16

Another Wayward Pig

*Above all, love each other deeply, because love
covers over a multitude of sins.*
—1 Peter 4:8 (NIV)

An incident occurred the same weekend where we had all these people at our house. As my daughter and I were in one of the outside pigpens, Braiden went into the kennel to see Pork Chop and Bacon Bit. The next thing I heard was a lot of squealing, and I saw a little black pig running from the kennel. Then I saw Braiden running behind the very small black pig. Pigs are so fast. I never knew how fast they were until I got pigs. It is the craziest thing. If you have never seen how fast a baby pot-belly pig can run, look up a video. It is so hilarious.

Back to the story. Jodie and I run out of the pen. I was frantic and screaming about making sure the pigpens were locked in all the craziness. So now we were all chasing the pig. I was not sure which one it was, did not matter, we had to catch this pig. These two pigs were too small to make it on their own in the woods. This pig did not go to the woods, he was running to the field. That situation could have been worse, in my head anyway. I was panicking like I have a tendency to do with these animals. Ronnie said, "Daisy, get the pig." Daisy went right for the pig. In the minute, the pig turned to go into the field, Daily was able to redirect the pig to get away from the field and back toward the house. The pig ran up to the porch with Daisy right behind. Ronnie was able to dive on the ground to grab the pig. Whew. What a workout.

Turns out, it was Pork Chop that ran away. He saw an opportunity because someone he did not know was in his pen and the door was not closed all the way. Pigs are extremely smart. In research, it shows pigs are smarter than dogs or cats and have mental capability of a two-year-old child. Pork Chop enjoyed his run but also enjoyed the cuddling to help him calm down. That is the one time he enjoyed being held. I may have enjoyed it more than him, but it does not really matter. I got him back into the pen with his sister who was very upset he was gone. They cuddled in the straw when I got him back in the pen. To date, he has never run away again. Thank goodness, I am not sure I was up for a second wayward pig in this bunch.

I guess it is funny, Pork Chop and Treat are my only two runaways. Spam and Bacon Bit neither one have tried to run away. Even if the gate is a little bit opened, they have not tried to leave. Even not liking me, they have not tried to leave.

Since getting into the bigger pens, Treat is so happy, she has not tried to escape again. She has decided that this is her home and does not want to leave again. Pork Chop is the same way. He does not want to leave. These pigs are happy.

CHAPTER 17

Loving Animals

*For every animal of the forest is mine, and cattle on a
thousand hills. I know every bird in the mountains,
and the insects in the fields are mine.*
—Psalm 50:10–11 (NIV)

One of the most fun things for me on the farm is having visitors here, seeing the looks on people's faces when the animals accept the new person. When the animals choose to accept someone, they light up, and they start to become somewhat animated. They return the love they are receiving. Each animal has a different way of doing this.

Cracker Jack comes to the fence and will allow someone to pet him, and he will move his head back and forth to show he is okay with it. Hercules will do something ornery, like a headbutt or untying a shoe, or breaking buttons on a shirt. This is to show he accepts you and wants someone to pet him and just love him. Romeo will keep walking past to ensure he gets seen and at least a pat on the head. He likes to bleat at people to get attention. Lucky does not want any part of any of it, so he stands back and watches. If you watch him long enough, he looks like he really wants to get some love and attention, but he is so scared.

Treat and Spam are still standoffish, but they will run around the pen and put on a good show. Gus comes right up to the gate almost begging for someone to pet him. He leans in human touch because he loves it so much. Pork Chop and Bacon Bit run to the back of the pen and hide unless you are my dad. For some reason, the little bitty pigs would let my dad pet them through the fence. He is the only person in the early days they would willingly let touch them at all.

The animals all learned early on when there are visitors, there are also lots of treats. Cracker Jack, Hercules, Romeo, and Lucky would usually get leaves from the tree bent over. Someone has to get into the pen for them to get this. They would also get stuff from my grandma's garden. The pigs would get vegetables or cheerios for treats. I am still new with the animals here but learning something new every day. It is so amazing to see all these new things. I wish I had known this years ago.

I do want to mention something here: my dad was there when Cracker Jack was loaded and brought home. Cracker Jack remembers my dad, and every time my dad comes over, Cracker Jack comes to the fence and wants to see him. It is really cute. Animals remember people, and they know who has good intentions for them. It amazes me how smart they are.

There have been several friends, family, and even people I did not really know that have come by to see the animals. Previous owners of the animals will come by to check up on them. It warms my heart that so many people do care about them. They will definitely make you smile and forget what stress you have in that moment.

CHAPTER 18

Pork Chop's Surgery

Trust in the Lord and do good; dwell in the land and enjoy safe pasture.
—Psalm 37:3 (NIV)

In my research, I discovered pigs mature quickly. They are able to start reproducing at three to four months of age. Pork Chop and Bacon Bit were coming up on that age, so I knew it was time to get Pork Chop fixed. I needed to get both of them fixed, but Pork Chop came first. The pigs were starting to get bigger. They were having some decrease in some appetite lately due to the heat. I knew it was time to do other things for them, but the neuter was the first thing on the list.

I got him to the vet. Poor Bacon Bit was not happy being left alone in the kennel, but it had to be done. I went on to work. I picked up Pork Chop on the way home, he did great in surgery. The vet did tell me he needed to be able to rest for a couple days so he could heal. I decided I would make him a place in the house since it was so hot outside.

I made Pork Chop a place in the laundry room. I put the crate in there and put down pads for him to use if he needed to go to the bathroom. He was so scared to be in the house without Bacon Bit. I thought I would be smart and bring Bacon Bit inside to help calm Pork Chop down. I put down more blankets on the floor for them both. Bringing Bacon Bit in did not calm him down, now they were both upset. They tore up all the pads and poured out the water all over the blankets and the food. The two pigs were huddled up in the corner scared to death.

My heart was broken. I hated this all so much for these poor babies. I wanted them to start to open up, but it was not happening.

I had a decision to make. What was I going to do? I could not bear to watch this the rest of the night. I knew the sun was going down, so the heat would not be as bad. I made the decision to put them back outside. I really did not want to do that since Pork Chop had literally just had surgery, but what choice did I have? They were miserable in the house.

I got them back outside in the pen, one at a time, of course. Once they were back in the pen, they cuddled up together in the straw, and they were fine. They knew they were fine. They were safe in their own home. That is what they knew, and this is what they wanted. They got what they wanted. They are spoiled pigs.

I think part of the reason they were so scared was because the dogs and the cats were really wanting to play with them. I had them blocked off and apart so there would not be any trouble with any of them, but that did not work. Just having other animals close to them scared them. I cannot say I blame them.

CHAPTER 19

The New Pen

For with God nothing shall be impossible.
—Luke 1:37 (KJV)

Pork Chop had just been neutered and still recovering from surgery. He and Bacon Bit were still in the kennel, and it was almost one hundred degrees outside. Since we had never had animals on the farm in the summer, we did not realize there was absolutely no ventilation in there in the kennel. The pigs were still very small, but their appetites had started to decrease, and it looked like they had been using the water bowl as a pool to cool off. I started noticing how miserable they were. Ronnie would not be home for two weeks. I was nervous to wait that long to get them out of that kennel. Pigs do not sweat, so I needed to do something for Pork Chop and Bacon Bit, so I did not lose them. But what? I am still new at this, and I am here alone.

I could not let my fear get to me. I just had to get something done for these babies. There was a pen next to the pen that Spam, Treat, and Gus were in. It did not look good, but we had planned to use it for these little guys. The weeds had already been killed in there, and the old doghouse had been burned. I decided to just rig it up the best I could to keep them in the pen outside and to get them out of that kennel.

I went by the store before going home to get what I needed to make this happen. I got a medium size doghouse and a couple more bowls for food and water. I called my husband to see where all the tools and things I needed were. He was very shocked when I told him what I was doing, but as always, he was supportive.

I had not really looked closely at the pen. When I started looking, I decided the babies could not crawl through since it was chicken wire (not the best thing to use for pigs) and not hog panels. The gate was busted, and there were some holes in places. I was not sure what I was doing, but I was determined to do it.

I got the doghouse set up and the bowls set out. Ronnie had bought railroad ties when fixing the first pen, and we had a few railroad ties left. I am a big girl, but doing that alone was not going to happen. I called my husband to get the secret to moving the railroad tie by myself. He told me to use a strap around the railroad tie to move it. Guess what? It worked. I was able to move that railroad tie to block the hole in the fencing so the pigs could not get out. I was so excited. Now to fix the gate, all that took was a bungee strap to hold it in place until something else could be done. I had done it. I had rigged it up enough to get the little pigs out of that miserably hot kennel.

I had done this not a minute too soon. It was ninety-five degrees, and the pigs were a little lethargic already. It was supposed to hit one hundred degrees the next day. I was so grateful to get them out of there. I got them out of there one at a time. They were running around and rooting and having the best time. It was like all the happiness in them came out all at once. It was amazing to see this.

The next day, I came home, and as always, I went to feed and water the animals. It was so hot out. The little pigs had rooted a spot behind the doghouse in the shade to stay cool. It was really cute. They had so much more room, and they were doing so much better already.

Pork Chop and Bacon Bit still did not like me much and were not warming up very fast, but this was a start. They would give me the stink eye when I would sit in the pen while they ate. They were so nervous. I really hated that for them. It had to get better.

CHAPTER 20

Animals and the Sixth Sense

Are not two sparrows sold for a penny? Yet not one of them
will fall to the ground outside your Father's care.
—Matthew 10:29

One thing that amazes me about these animals is the compassion they have for each other. I have never seen anything like it. I have written about my dog, Maggie, having a seizure disorder, and she is a ten-year-old. She is doing well right now with her medication. She has not had any more seizures lately. Cracker Jack is a fourteen-year-old donkey. He really hates Daisy, but she is a puppy, fast and wild. She likes to run to the fence and scares him. Maggie just walks the fence line with Cracker Jack. Cracker Jack makes sure to go to the fence. They will walk the fence back and forth like they are best friends. It is adorable to watch. Cracker Jack loves Pepper also but more so Maggie. I feel like Cracker Jack knows she is sick and is trying to show her some love and compassion.

On the flip side of that, Daisy and the goats are the exact opposite. Those goats try to headbutt that dog. She will then grab their horns with her teeth. It looks like they are fighting, but they are really just playing. It sure does look aggressive.

I have let Pepper in the pen with the donkey and goats. Cracker Jack and Pepper just kind of circled each other for a while. The goats wanted nothing to do with her. It was a little uneventful. I have not done this again for fear of Hercules getting to her with his horns.

CHAPTER 21

Progress

In the morning, Lord, you hear my voice; in the morning
I lay my requests before you and wait expectantly.
—Psalm 5:3 (NIV)

I went out to see Pork Chop and Bacon Bit. I thought I was making some progress because Bacon Bit ran to the fence to see me. Once she saw me, she ran away. I guess she remembered she did not like me. She must have forgotten for just a minute.

I went in to see my one and only friendly pig, Gus. I was petting him and loving on him. The other two, Spam and Treat, were starting to see the attention Gus was getting, and they were starting to become more friendly. When I said becoming more friendly, it was definitely going slow, but I was able to pet them occasionally.

Gus was so friendly now. I was out in the pen, and he actually gave me Eskimo kisses. I did not know they could do that. I was so shocked. These pigs amaze me every single day. I had no idea how much these pigs would get into my heart. They got into my heart and started filling some cracks I was not aware I had.

To help with the progress of the two little pigs, Bacon Bit and Pork Chop, I started sitting on the ground with treats. I will put the treats out right in front of me so they get closer to me. I finally reached out and touched Pork Chop's head, and he squealed up a storm. I sat there for hours talking to them and just being there for them to get used to. I was so glad Pork Chop and Bacon Bit came here together. Since I spent so much time with them, I was seeing they would not have done well apart. They needed each other.

The bigger pigs—Spam, Gus, and Treat—must have started to get used to me. I walked into the pen one day while they were all asleep. I went in and started talking to them. I startled them, and they all jumped up and ran in all different directions trying to get out of the pen. Poor Gus even ran right into the fence. I laughed so hard after I checked on him.

Gus did a belly flop. The first time he did this, I thought he was hurt. All of a sudden, Gus just fell over. This is to show me he wanted his belly rubbed. When I figured out what he was doing, I gave him all the belly rubs he wanted. He is such a sweet boy. When he does the roll over thing, the other two come over to check on him, and they get closer to me so I can pet them.

I did attempt to hand-feed the big pigs. Gus does fine. Spam and Treat were not ready for that. Treat did okay, but she was not too sure about it. Spam bit me, and it bled and bled. I will not make that mistake again. I do see this as progress, though. Something is better than nothing.

I know progress takes a while. I am writing this story now, but this all takes place almost a year ago. Up until now, these stories all have taken place in a three-month period. In my research, I have read potbelly pigs can live up to twenty years; this means I have plenty of time to get them socialized.

CHAPTER 22

Learning Curve

Guide me in your truth and teach me, for you are God
my Savior, and my hope is in you all day long.
—Psalm 25:5 (NIV)

I need to remember that I am still learning how to do things on this farm. I should not be so hard on myself when I make mistakes. I noticed Hercules had started losing his hair. I did not know what was happening. I was starting to get nervous. It could have been lice, rubbing the fence, fungus, or a mineral deficiency. I did not know which it was. I did not think it was lice since the other goats did not have it. I got a new mineral block for them because I ruled out everything but the mineral deficiency. The mineral block helped with the hair loss.

Here is the mistake I made. When I went to get a mineral block, I might have gotten the wrong one. I did not really look at the types of mineral blocks, I just looked for the mineral that Hercules was deficient in. Trust me, I did a lot of research to figure it out. I was trying to be independent on getting what we needed without asking. I got home, and as I unwrapped it and threw it over the fence, it was actually a mineral block for reproductive health. They were already eating it like their lives depended on it.

When I was telling Ronnie about it, he could not stop laughing about it. It really is funny. The goats were all fine, nothing out of the ordinary even with the mineral block. Around this time, the lady we got the goats from called and said she needed to rehome some of her female goats. That made the reproductive block even funnier. I did decline the offer, though. I did not need a bunch of babies running around even if they were the cutest little things.

I am still learning and made another mistake. I am still doing a lot of research on pigs, and I think I am getting information in my head and then panicking. It had been raining a little bit but just a small shower that day. I came home from work and went to feed and water all the animals. I was doing the chores, and I looked up at Gus, and he had all these dark spots on him. I panicked.

I had been reading about dippity pig syndrome. This is a syndrome caused by stress in pigs. They break out in sores on their back, and they start to have difficulty with their back legs. It sounded awful. Gus does not seem to have any of the symptoms, except the dark spots, but they are everywhere not just on his back. I posted a picture on social media on my pig asking for advice. I really felt like an idiot when someone posted back to me that my pig had wet spots on him from the rain and only had dry skin. I was so relieved that nothing was wrong with him, but I need to stop panicking.

I have also learned during this string of mistakes is to be careful when worming a goat. Romeo has an awful time with worms. He is the only one that seems to have such a bad problem. Ronnie got a drench gun to help worm the goats. The first time we tried to use it, I grabbed his horns to hold him as Ronnie gave him the meds. Well, as Ronnie put the drench gun in Romeo's mouth, Romeo moved and stabbed me in the chest with a horn. Okay, that does not feel good. About the same time, I got stabbed, the drench gun came apart, and Romeo almost swallowed part of it. Ronnie caught it in time. That could have been a bad thing to happen.

With me growing up in the city, I had not had to deal with mice much in a house. I was not aware after the hay was cut in a field, the mice seemed to come into the house. I am seeing that my cats are not good mousers. I have only seen a couple, and they get removed from the house. The mistake here is that I was not aware of the possibility of a mouse in the house. It is a good thing I do not panic about them. I pick them up and put them outside. I just cannot kill them. I did this one time, and I picked up the mouse, and the mouse was scared, but I was able to pet it and put it outside. The very next day, this happened again, but this mouse was not so friendly and almost bit me. I did get it outside also. I was telling Ronnie the story, and he laughed and said something like, "It is cold outside, and it was probably the same mouse from yesterday and is now made about you putting it outside." Then I had to laugh. I would be mad, too, if someone kept throwing me outside.

CHAPTER 23

Funny Pigs

Take delight in the Lord, and he will give you the desires of your heart.
—Psalm 37:4

I am going to try to give you a clear picture on how funny these pigs are. It is unbelievable how much they make me laugh. The joy surrounding them is indescribable. Each one of them has a different personality and mannerisms. Every one of them has been through so much, but they are sweet animals who are trying to trust me. They are working on it.

One day, I was out in the pigpen, and Gus was sleeping in my lap. All of a sudden, Gus jumped out of my lap and started barking like a dog. I could not believe my ears, a pig barking like a dog. I had no idea what was happening. Then I saw Daisy running by the pen, and it all made sense after that. Daisy loved to hang out at the pigpen. Maybe she taught Gus to bark.

Another night, I had had a very long day, and I was exhausted. I was not in a good mood, but I had chores to do. I was the only one there, so I had to get it done. I had finally finished the chores and sat down to see Gus. Gus came over for a few minutes. Treat did not want anything to do with me. However, Spam came toward me. When she realized what she was doing, she changed her mind really quickly and ran off. I had to laugh at her.

A couple nights later, I was sitting on the ground with Treat, Gus, and Spam, and the girls had started coming closer to me. Treat started biting at my pants. I had nothing in my pockets, so I had no idea what she was doing. When I tried to pet her, she ran off like crazy. I think she wanted so badly for me to pet her, but she still was not sure of me. She was the one that started this crazy love for pigs. I feel she should know by now I was not going to hurt her.

Ronnie was outside mowing in the heat of a summer day. He was warming up to the pigs. He would call the razorback hogs every time he would pass the pigpens. The pigs would all bark back at him, all five of the pigs. It was so funny to watch. They did this for at least an hour with him.

Out in the big pigpen (that is the pen with Gus, Treat, and Spam), I was watching Treat while loving on Gus. Treat picked up a stick and started running around with it. She was absolutely adorable. Spam tried to take the stick from Treat, and she was not having it. She started grunting at Spam. I can only imagine what she was saying. Spam actually let Treat keep the stick. I think she just lost interest because if Spam really wanted it, she would have taken it without a problem. Poor Treat, she is smaller than Spam. Spam is a mean sister sometimes.

Gus has started a bad habit. When I go into the pen and I do not get the food in the bowl fast enough, he starts rooting on my leg. Those noses are so strong. He continues until I drop the food for him. It is funny because he is so spoiled. I have so many bruises on my legs that my husband asked me not to wear shorts. He said it looked like he had been kicking me or something. I assure you, I am not a battered woman. I have a fantastic husband.

Cracker Jack has quite the personality also. I was in that pen with him and the goats, and all of a sudden, Cracker Jack got on the ground and started rolling on his back in the grass. I could not believe my eyes. I had never seen such a thing in my life. When he got up and looked at me, it was like he was saying, "What are you looking at?" I had an itch, but it was gone now. The funniest thing about this was, I thought he was hurt for a minute. Nope, I was overreacting again.

My big pigs started acting like they did not like the mud. They acted like they were disgusted by it, tiptoeing around it. They were pulling one over on me. When I was not watching them, they were all three playing in it and were then muddy form head to toe. They also would not let me give them a bath.

The bugs down here in Arkansas in the middle of summer are brutal. Mosquitoes are everywhere. I thought it would be a good idea to put bug spray on the pigs to keep the ticks and mosquitoes off them. Of course, Gus was the only one that would allow me to spray him. The girls were having flashbacks of the frontline spray when they had mange. After I sprayed Gus down, Treat decided she liked the spray and started crawling on him. That was a hilarious sight to see. He did not pay any attention to her.

CHAPTER 24

Healthy Farm Animals or Not

Dear friend, I pray that you may enjoy good health and that all may go well with you, even as your soul is getting along well.
—3 John 1:2

I had been noticing Cracker Jack had been getting all these mysterious cuts on his legs. I could not figure out where or how he was getting them. There were new ones every day. I would go out and try to doctor them for him. He really hated it, but he tolerated me. The goats did not have any cuts on them. I was confused. I finally figured it out. One day, it was superhot out. Cracker Jack got into the bushes in the pen to stay cool. In the bushes were several areas of stumps where he was getting the cuts. The mystery was finally solved. It stopped happening when the weather cooled off. In this time, there were a lot of moments of doctoring cuts.

Maggie became really sick during the first summer we had the farm. She had so much going on with the seizures and the possible brain tumor. Some days were just really rough on her. One weekend, I got up, and she had been vomiting in the middle of the night. She had been limping for several days before this, but I did not think much of it.

I started checking her over but did not see anything. Once she started vomiting, she could not stop. Maggie had even started to throw up blood which was a scary sight. She did not want to eat. It was even hard to get her to drink anything because it would not stay with her. I stayed on the floor with her and just cried while I held her. She was getting old, but I was not ready to let her go.

As sick as she was, it got to the point Ronnie and I thought we were going to have to make some decisions. I finally rechecked her paw, and it looked like she had been bitten by a snake. I am still not sure that is what happened, but that is what it looked like. A few days after this started, it just stopped, and Maggie was so much better. I cried so much and prayed so much those few days for Maggie. She beat the illness. God was still with us. He was showing me that with the animals more than I could ever tell you.

The smaller pigs, Bacon Bit and Pork Chop, were not growing much. They were around four months old and still were very small. They were very picky eaters. They had been eating some pellets and grazing on grass before they came home with me, they did not like the change in feed. They love corn, but that is not healthy for them. I learned that at some point after having five potbelly pigs. I finally decided I had to do something. I got some baby cereal and mixed that with water and pumpkin, added some pellets, and they ate it. I did not have anymore difficulty with those babies eating. They even would eat off the spoon. It was a really hilarious sight.

One night, I was doing my last check of the animals for the night. I noticed Spam was having some urinary issues. I panicked. Why would I not? Apparently, that is what I do. Ronnie did not say a word. He knew I was panicking. Ronnie and I ran to the store right before the store closed and got a broad-spectrum antibiotic since I thought she probably had an infection. When we got back and got in the pen with the bigger pigs to give Spam a shot, well, we figured out very quickly that shot was not going to happen. She ran around the pen screaming. During this time, we both decided she was fine. I got up early the next morning to see her trying to climb a fence because she was in heat. That is what the whole issue was. The antibiotic did not have to be given.

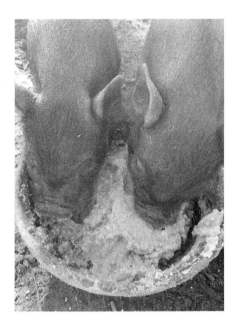

Now let me tell you what I have had to deal with. Poor Romeo. He ended up getting coccidiosis. I thought that was some made up disease, but it was not. I went out to the pen one day, and the poor goat had had such diarrhea that it was literally running down the back of his legs. I felt so terrible for him. This went on for days. Of course, he was cleaned up, but it continued to happen. I bought me a book to help me with learning (I bought one on goats, donkeys, and potbelly pigs). I was looking up the symptoms Romeo had, and it definitely looked like coccidiosis. So Ronnie went and got some medicine to treat Romeo. The entire herd had to be treated also. The medicine worked, and we have not had another problem with this.

While I was trying to figure out what was going on with Romeo, I called the lady I got him from. She was not sure what was going on with him, but she did tell me that his sister had a lot of problems with worms like Romeo did. It was almost like he had them most of the time, even with treated. I went back and forth between worming medicine so he did not get immune to a worming medicine, which did happen. She did recommend for me not to breed him because it seemed like it was a genetic thing. I was not going to breed him anyway, but it was good to know. I did take extra time checking on Romeo to make sure he did not have worms. That poor goat. He sure was a happy goat, though. He really was a great little goat. He was so loving and sweet.

CHAPTER 25

Progress Being Made

Therefore, my beloved brothers, be steadfast, immovable,
always abounding in the work of the Lord, knowing
that in the Lord your labor is not in vain.
—1 Corinthians 15:58 (ESV)

As you have read so far, I love these animals. They have truly been healing for me to have them here. I rescued most of them, but they really rescued me. I think that is an important part of the story. I did not know I needed rescuing. I did not know what was happening to me. I was so happy. Not that I was not happy before, but it looked like I still needed some healing in areas I did not know were an issue. I had a great life before these animals, but somehow, they were making it even better.

Treat and Spam were the first pigs here, and they had been through so much before getting here and after getting here due to pneumonia and mange. I have not mentioned that this was actually their third home in the first few months of their lives. The progress with them was slow. They were very scared of people. I continued to sit with them and give them treats. I would sit on the ground so I would not scare them. Gus was in that pen also. This was also his third home. He was showing Treat and Spam what it looked like to get attention. They were starting to get curious.

By now, Spam and Treat were letting me pet them but just for a second usually. Treat was warming up faster than Spam. What most people do not know about pigs is they have good memories. Since they have good memories, they can have trust issues. You have to break down their walls for them to trust you. This is a lot like humans. It is a slow process for some pigs depending on where they have been in their lives.

I was out in the pen one day sitting on the ground. I was giving Gus some attention. He loves belly rubs and kisses on the nose. I did not realize Spam and Treat were watching so closely to what he had been doing, but they had. At least Treat had been paying attention. On this particular evening in the hot summer, Treat walked up to where I was sitting and wanted me to pet her. I started petting her carefully so I would not scare her. She actually let me pet her for a long time without running away. I could not believe my eyes. I was so excited. I had been waiting for months for this.

When I stopped petting Treat so I could go inside, I got up and leaned over her to try to kiss her cute little nose. I really thought she would run away, but she did not run away. My sweet, wayward pig let me kiss her nose. This was a huge step here. I was so happy. She had been here for four months and was finally realizing she was safe here and could be happy here. I had started breaking down the walls for her to trust me.

Spam was really trying. She would let me per her a little bit, but she was still really nervous around me. If I stayed around her too long, she would snap and try to bite me. I would try to love on her as long as I could before she snapped. I was determined.

Now that Treat and Spam were getting some attention, Gus decided he did not like this. He became jealous of the attention he was not getting. He would come up to me to get in the middle of me petting the other two. This was his way of getting what he wanted. I gave him belly rubs and kisses. He was so jealous; he snapped at me and almost got me in the face. I am glad I have good reflexes. I petted on him after that as an apology, and he seemed good. He still does this on occasions.

A couple of weeks after Treat was starting to get friendly with me, Spam started warming up. Spam has always been the protector of Treat. I think that is why she has been so difficulty to get to open up. She was now the only one in that pen that was not getting any attention, and she wanted in on that. Spam had decided I was okay to pet her. She finally did a belly flop for me so I could rub her belly. This was such a big deal for her. I took it a little far and tried to kiss her nose, but she snapped. She would have taken my face off. I will not be doing that for a while again. She continued to love belly rubs, so we stopped there.

Spam did start to get the jealous bug from Gus, though. Once she decided she liked to have her belly rubbed and liked to get attention, she was going to get her attention. I was sitting with them in the pen on the ground, and Treat did a belly flop for a belly rub. Spam charged at her and missed her but bit me instead. I do not think she really did it on purpose. She did get me, though. It only bled for a second, and it was really just a scratch. I did make sure to clean it and watched for infection just in case. Looking back, I find it funny that she wanted to get that belly rub bad enough to attack Treat but missed her. I could tell she felt bad because she came up to me with some apologetic eyes. I could not even be mad at her.

The little pigs, Pork Chop and Bacon Bit, still were not warming up quickly. By now, we had added two more little pigs to the pen, Patsy and Brutus. That is a whole other book in itself. None of those little pigs wanted any attention. However, they would eat out of my hand. They did not want to be touched, though, so it took a lot of patience with them. I still sat out there on the ground with them and talked softly to them. Time, love, and patience are what it takes to get pigs to warm up to you. When they do, it feels like you have made the progress you were hoping for. My heart was so full.

Since Spam, Treat, and Gus all are finally letting me pet them and give belly rubs and kisses (minus Spam in the kisses), they all fight for my attention. The new challenge is the snapping at me because of jealousy. Spam is the worst about this. I cannot turn my back on her to pet Treat or Gus because she will try to bite me. I do not believe it is out of aggression, but it is out of jealousy. Gus will do this also on occasion when jealous. They do not make me nervous, but I am cautious of them. I have an eye out for all three of them at all times. Treat is my sweet one, she has not snapped at me so far.

The progress with these animals is truly an astounding thing to watch. Some people may say I am out of my mind, but I want them to have the best life possible. I know I spend a crazy amount of time with them, but if I did not spend all that time with them, I would have not made the progress I have made. I have made so much progress with them. Gus will even start to put when it starts to get dark out and I have to go inside. Yes, I said pout. He will turn his back to me, and he will lay on the ground with his head down. It is sad but adorable at the same time. I knew dogs did this, but I had not seen a pig do this. All in all, things are looking up.

Well, Lucky finally let me pet him. I find that as progress also. He is still not friendly. He is actually still very skittish. I feel so bad for him. He wants to be loved on so badly. I could see it in his eyes. I went to the fence one day with a handful of food, and he actually ate out of my hand. That is how it started. I am able to now pet him on his head but only if I am on the other side of the fence. If I go in the fence, I can forget it. I still have hope, though. I think he will get there. It might take so much longer than I thought it would, but it will get there. I feel it in my bones.

CHAPTER 26

Antics on the Farm

The grasslands of the wilderness overflow; the hills are clothed
with gladness. The meadows are covered with flocks and the
valleys are mantled with grain; they shout for joy and sing.
—Psalm 65:12–13 (NIV)

The goats had another bad case of worms. I know worms come
from eating the grass from the ground. Lucky was still not friendly

and refused to come to any of us. I knew he needed to be wormed along with the rest of them. Ronnie decided he would rope him so we could get meds in him.

This is not to hurt him in any way. He needed that medicine, and there was no other way to do it. Ronnie tried a few times, but Lucky was too fast. He was having none of it. In fact, he hid in the bushes where we could not get him. He did not get the medicine. I fed him some worming pellets and prayed it would work. I guess it did because he was still doing fine and his belly did not look like it did. Keep in mind, I am still new at this, and I am having to do trial and error with these things.

One thing out of about a million I did not know is pigs need grass for their digestive systems. I was feeding them pig pellets, hay, and occasionally corn. Corn is not good for them and makes them fat. My babies love it, so I would give it to them one meal out of the week. I do not do this anymore because I do not want them to get fat or sick from what I am feeding them. I have a say, but they do not.

There was no grass in their pens because they had literally rooted it all up. When I learned they needed grass, I tried to plant some in the pens. They rooted that up as soon as it started to grow. Good thing they are cute.

My mom was over one day when Ronnie and I were cleaning up the yard and mowing. She said to try to give them the grass we cut. My mom and I started gathering up and putting in buckets to save for the pigs. I started throwing some over the fence for them. Those pigs went crazy. They fought over that grass and ate it up quickly. Who would have thought?

Pigs love belly rubs, and as you know, my little pigs are not friendly yet during this point in the story. I was out by the pens, and all of a sudden, I saw one of the pigs on their side, I think it was Bacon Bit with Brutus rubbing her belly with his nose. It was the funniest thing to watch.

The sad part of it is, I think Brutus was still so young and he was actually wanting to nurse. I am not positive on this thought, but that is what it looked like to me. He did this for several more months after he came to live here. It was cute, though.

Pigs fight for food. They just do. It does not matter that they are bonded, they still fight for the food. I had started watching the pigs during feeding time. I noticed it was a game for them. I gave them all food in their own bowl, and then they would switch. After they switched, they would switch again. They would do this until all the food was gone. It was like watching musical bowls without the music. It was actually hilarious. It does come with some problems, with more fighting, but that is what pigs do.

Cracker Jack is spoiled like no other. He has started braying constantly until someone comes out and gives him food. He starts extremely early in the morning. He does this every hour on the hour basically until he gets what he wants. It does get old sometimes hearing all that all the time when he loves to eat grass, but he has to have that hay in the morning. He does not stop until he gets his hay.

Another silly antic Cracker Jack does is when people come over, he brays to alert us someone is here that he does not know. It actually scares people sometimes. To me, it is funny to see the looks on their faces. He is my security for the house.

One specific instance this happened, my cousin was at the house before I got home from work. I parked in the front of the house where she did not see me pull in the driveway. She was cleaning the pool for me. Where she was standing, all she knew was the donkey was braying and she did not know why. I walked around the corner to see my cousin standing there looking nervous. Props to her for not falling into the pool. She said she had no idea what was going on. I had to laugh.

In the heat of the summer, the pigs want to stay cool. Pork Chop tries to root under the water bowls and ends up dumping it out. He also tries to fit in the water bowl, it does not work. He falls out with the water bowl on top of him. Spam has done the same thing. Ronnie got them pools, those little kid pools, and put them in the pens. That helped quite a bit to keep them cool. Pigs do not sweat, so it is very important for pigs to stay cool in the hot weather.

There is a little problem with the pools in the pen. The instinct of a pig is to use the water as a bathroom. I have to clean these pools out daily. As long as they are cool in the hundred-degree weather, it is okay with me. Like I said, pigs do not sweat, so it can be dangerous if they cannot cool off. I do not want them to have any heat strokes.

Animals love routine. They know when it is time for me to be out there to feed them and love on them. All them—donkey, goats, and pigs—they are all lined up by the fences waiting on me. Usually, the donkey is braying, the goats are bleating, and the pigs are screaming. Sometimes, I think they might be happy to see me. Other times, I think they all just want food.

Ronnie bought me a wagon to be able to put the buckets of water in to transport them instead of carrying them. I never thought I would be doing any of this farming stuff. It is such hard work. The night he got me the wagon, we tied the wagon to the back of the truck, and he pulled me around in the yard. It was so fun, but the animals were all wondering what was going on. The dogs were trying to follow. That is how we have fun on the farm.

Romeo is such a hilarious goat. I was spending some time with the goats in the pen. Romeo loves me, and he wants to be around me. I was petting on him, and he came up to my face. I thought he was going to be sweet, so I put my arms around him like in a hugging motion, and he accepted the hug but bit my face during the hug. Needless to say, he did not really want that hug.

Another night, I was trying to take selfies with Romeo. He is usually a very good sport about the selfies. This night, he was really liking those selfies. He decided he would take his own selfie. I kid you not, this goat walked up to the phone and hit the button with his nose. I will never forget this because I could not stop laughing. I am sure he thought it was another goat or something he needed to get to know, but it was just my phone. This was too funny.

Another little antic here on the farm is the full moon. I know there is not much we can do about the moon, but the stories about people doing out of character things are not just in people, animals do out of character things also. Cracker Jack refuses to sleep in the shelter when there is a full moon. The dogs do not want to stay home. The pigs seem to fight more and are more skittish than normal, the little pigs do this. The bigger pigs seem more aggressive than normal when there is a full moon. I wish I could make this stuff up. It is really wild around here when there is a full moon.

I mentioned the pools a little while back. On a hot day, Spam and Gus will fight over the pool. There is enough room in there for both of them, but they will not get in there together. If Gus was in there, Spam would scream at him. When Spam was in there, Gus would scream at her. It was a hot day but good grief. Poor Treat, she will not even attempt to get in there since the other two are awful to each other and she does not want any part of that.

CHAPTER 27

The Next Rescue

*Are not two sparrows sold for a cent? And yet not one of
them will fall to the ground apart from your Father.*
—Matthew 10:29 (NIV)

I have mentioned Patsy and Brutus already, so I need to tell you
about their rescue. By this time, I had learned so much about pigs
and the pig population problems with potbelly pigs. I got a call from
the breeder I had picked up Pork Chop and Bacon Bit from. He said
he was overrun with pigs, and he needed to get rid of them. I discussed it with Ronnie. He laughed since we already had five of them.

I called the guy back and asked him if he had any females, and he said he had one, so I told him I would take that one female. Notice, I said one. Keep that in mind. I scheduled a time to pick her up.

I went a few days later to pick her up. She was a terrified little pig in a pen alone. I hated to see her like that. She was so scared. They had seven more male pigs they needed to get rid of before the next litter was due. I was determined to only take one pig, but my heart was breaking. I did not need that one pig, so I sure did not need more than one. The guy told me he might have to dump the babies, so I should take all I could. My heart completely shattered in that moment. I am not sure he would to that or not, but it broke me apart.

As I was leaving with the new pig, we now call Patsy, the smallest pig I had even seen ran past me. I asked about the tiny pig and what was going to happen to him. The man told me he was hoping someone would take him. This tiny pig was the runt of the litter. He was so tiny. I am sure you know what I did: I brought him home. I had one small animal carrier with me, and both of these pigs fit into this one small carrier. I hope that shows how small they were. My heart would not let me leave him. He was so tiny, so he needed a big name. I wanted to name him Winston. My husband came up with Brutus. Brutus fit him well. His name became Brutus. This was definitely not in my plans, but that is what happened anyway. I actually still think about the pigs I left behind. It still breaks my heart to think about it.

I got Patsy and Brutus home and had to endure watching the introductions to Pork Chop and Bacon Bit. It was not as bad as I had seen with the other pigs, but it still was not fun to watch. I made sure I bought more bowls and another doghouse for them. That was to decrease the fighting, and it did work a little. The one thing that I did see was Bacon Bit actually picking Brutus up with her nose and throwing him in the air. She was not very big at the time, so it really showed how small Brutus really was.

All the fighting and the being in a new environment really put Patsy in a deep depression. She was not eating much, and she was lying in the corner of the pen. It was so sad to see. Brutus would go over and lay down with her to comfort her. This went on for weeks. I was really getting worried about her. I was happy I brought Brutus home also. I do not think Patsy would have made it here without him.

I did not ask Ronnie about getting both Patsy and Brutus. I did tell him later, and he laughed about it. He figured I would do something like that. I sent him pictures of the new pigs. He does not get excited about things, but he was excited to meet Brutus. Brutus was so tiny and looked nothing like the rest of the pigs. This made me so happy.

I am not sure Brutus was not so happy about going with me the first day. I was so curious about this pig because he was so small. I had never seen anything like it. I picked him up several times, and as you have read, that is not helpful. They really do hate that. Of course, he screamed like I was trying to hurt him, and he snapped at me after the last time, so I stopped picking him up. He was having enough difficulty with adjusting to the new home.

The pigs finally started to get along. The fighting had stopped. I was so grateful. Looks like Bacon Bit was top hop in the pen now. She is a beast in there. I went out one night to do my nightly routine check, and I could not find all the smaller pigs. I decided to not follow the rule about leaving sleeping animals alone, and I started yelling their names. Believe it or not, Patsy, Bacon Bit, and Pork Chop all ran out of one doghouse. Then I panicked. Where was Brutus? He was the only smart one. He stayed in that same doghouse the rest of them had left. They were all in there together. I could not believe my eyes. They were all getting along. It was so great to see.

The little pigs were starting to warm up to me some. The little pigs are Bacon Bit, Pork Chop, Patsy, and Brutus. Bacon Bit was now eating out of my hand. She would also try to suck on my fingers, which was so weird, but it showed progress. That was something. They were not screaming as I walked in the pen now.

The little pigs were watching me with the big pigs, and I think they were wanting my attention, but they were still afraid. When I talk about the big pigs, I am talking about Spam, Gus, and Treat. Patsy had started letting me pet her but only when she was eating.

She would run away otherwise. Brutus and Pork Chop are not as friendly, but it will come in time.

These pigs truly love routine. They know when I am supposed to out there, and they line up and wait. They scream while waiting, but they wait. Brutus heard me coming out of the door and started squealing like something was after him. I swear, he thinks he is starving, but he is not starving. He has started growing like a little weed. It is so adorable.

One thing I will mention is Brutus had not been fixed yet. I had called the vet, and they said he was too small and to call back when he was about four months old. I know pigs get mature at a very young age, between three to four months old. I knew Bacon Bit was getting to the age that she would be going into heat. I was getting nervous. I did not want to be part of the pig population problem. The day Brutus was old enough, I took him to get fixed.

The night before I got Brutus fixed, I had to put him in my bathtub. He was still too small to get out of that area. I took him in the next morning. He did fine in surgery. I picked him up, and since it was so hot out, I decided to keep him in the bathtub another night to help him heal. I was also being selfish and wanted to try to win him over. I cuddled him and loved on him. He finally just relaxed and let me cuddle him. When it was time to go to bed, I put him back in the bathtub.

The next morning, I got up to check on Brutus. He was throwing a fit. I brought him some food, but the fit continued. Now I had baby food and pumpkin everywhere in the tub. Turns out, Brutus would have been easy to potty train. He needed to use the bathroom. I know this is going to sound truly unbelievable, but he walked over to the bathtub drain and urinated. Seriously, I cannot make this stuff up. I had put pads down in the bathtub for him to use to go to the bathroom, but he would not do it. He would not calm down either, so I took him outside with his friends. That is what he wanted. He was fine after that. He was able to have a bowel movement when he went outside, so he was feeling better. The other pigs circled him to make sure he was okay.

A few months later, I was watching Bacon Bit. I have photos that look like she was pregnant and had an arm or a leg kicking her. Oh, I panicked, more so than I normally do. I sent pictures to the vet who said he thought she was pregnant also. I made an appointment with the vet to do an ultrasound to check. I knew she was so young, and it was scary to me. I did not want this to be happening. I was praying that this was not what it looked like.

I attempted to catch Bacon Bit the night before the appointment. That did not work. She was not having it. Ronnie came home that night and said he would help me in the morning. He did help me get her. I think it involved him tackling her to catch her. I kid you not.

I got Bacon Bit to the vet. She had an ultrasound. The vet was shaking his head. He said something like, "I really thought she was pregnant, but there are no babies in there." I have to tell you I was dumbfounded, and he seemed like it also. Good news was, Bacon Bit was not pregnant. Good grief, this farm is something else—always and adventure around here.

I will say this, Brutus finally decided he loves me. I was trying to pet him, which he does not want me to do. I put my hand through the fence, and he actually let me pet him. He even did a belly flop for me through the fence. I went in the fence for him to do a belly flop, but he wanted nothing to do with it.

I have not mentioned Patsy in a while. She is warming up. It is very slow with her. She worries me because she never looks well. She is slower than the other pigs on everything. She is trying, though. She is very sweet but very fearful. I give her space to warm up.

Pork Chop was doing fine also. I think he is still mad at me over being neutered. He refused to go around me. He does not seem to want to warm up. He only comes near me when I have treats or when I am on the other side of the fence.

CHAPTER 28

New Houses

*For behold, I create new heavens and a new earth; And the
former things will not be remembered or come to mind.*
—Isaiah 65:17 (KJV)

Things started turning cold out as fall/winter was upon us here in
Arkansas. I knew these pigs would not make it through the winter

in the doghouses or the lean-to. It was time to talk to my husband about new houses.

I talked Ronnie into building the pigs' new shelters for the cold weather. He did Spam, Treat, and Gus's new shelter. They absolutely love it. I put a bunch of straw in there to keep them warm and comfortable.

The next time Ronnie came home, he did the new shelter for the little pigs' pen. Those pigs did not like him in their pen. They watched his every move. When he moved one way, they all four moved in a different way. It was funny to watch them. Once it was finished, I put a bunch of straw in there, and those pigs were so happy.

Ronnie also added onto the lean to for the donkey and the goats. He wanted to make sure they would be warm in the winter. I added straw in there for them also. In doing that, at least the goats could get warmer.

Literally, the day after the last shelter was built, the nights got down to freezing. I was so glad they were all finished. There were mornings I would go out and I could not see the pigs because they were buried beneath the straw so far. They run out with straw still all over their heads. I cannot help but laugh at them over that. Picture it: little pigs running out of a shelter barking and oinking with straw still over their eyes. It is funny.

Ronnie also installed a light down at the pigpens. I was so terrified about coyotes getting in the pen and getting to the pigs. I was not worried about the donkey and the goats. I knew Cracker Jack would take care of that. He also put the light up since I was now feeding in the dark in the morning and at night. It helped a lot. I really was grateful for it.

These shelters were all rustic looking. They were so cute. I am so grateful my husband deals with all my farm antics. He does not get upset. He just does what needs to be done. Poor guy, he works on stuff for the animals all the time. They are needy, or I am. I just know they deserve the best care, and that is what they will get here.

CHAPTER 29

Another Goat Rescue

Then they cried out to the Lord I their trouble;
He saved them out of their distresses.
—Psalm 107:19 (NIV)

What am I doing? Remember my friend who called me about taking Gus? I ended up taking Gus, he was my fifth pig. Well, she called again. What do I do? I answered the phone. Out comes a story about a goat.

The story was, a friend of my friend's goats were attacked by a bobcat. One of the goats was killed but the bobcat. Sounds like the one that passed away was protecting the other one and that is how he made it. The family was nervous about another attack and wanted him to go to a good family. So I was called.

Okay, so at this point, I was up to three dogs, two cats, a donkey, three goats, and seven pigs. Would I be okay taking another animal? Would I be able to give another animal enough attention, the type of attention they all deserve? These are questions I think of each time I think about getting another animal. I need to make sure they are going to get the best are possible and this baby was injured.

I decided I would take the goat. He was an altered male, young, and his name was Carlos. We came up with a time for them to bring him to me. When he got to the house, I helped unload him and got him into the pen with the other goats and Cracker Jack. It was dark, and it was late, so I was not able to get a good look at him. I did have to keep the other goats off him. They seemed very excited to have a new goat in the pen. They surrounded him. Poor guy was terrified. I felt so bad for him. It was late, and I needed to get inside also. I just prayed Carlos would be okay through the night.

I got up the next morning to feed, but it was five o'clock in the morning, and it was still dark out. I was still not able to get a good look at him and his injuries. I was worried that I had not been able to see what we were dealing with. I knew the previous owner had given him antibiotics and he had started to heal. He was okay when I went out to feed. The other goats were still all around him, but he was able to eat fine also. There was hope here. Apparently, goats are not as brutal as pigs are with introductions. I am grateful for that since he was already injured.

My husband had gotten home around noon the day after Carlos came to the farm. I called him to ask him to check on Carlos. I knew I had told him we were getting another goat because he said something along the lines of, at least it was not another pig. So he went to check, and then I got a text. It went like this: "Have you seen this goat?"

I replied, "Not in the daylight."

He replied back, "Oh."

Then I asked if Carlos was okay, and he said he was doing okay. I left it alone after that, but I was really anxious to get home.

I made it home before dark by thirty minutes. I ran in the house to give my husband a kiss and ran back outside to see Carlos. Ronnie came with me. That made me nervous. He wanted to see my reaction. I did not care what the goat looked like as long as he was safe and accepted by the others.

I walked outside, and I saw them all, of course, around Carlos. The new kid on the block got all the attention. I got into the pen, and Carlos ran right up to me. It was almost like a "help me" look he had on his face and Lucky running right behind him. It was cute. Carlos was bleating at me the whole time. I finally got a good look at Carlos and his injuries.

There were several injuries to this poor goat. He was missing his entire left ear and half of his right ear. He also had been scratched down the center of his nose, so his nose was a little disfigured. He had puncture wounds in his sides. His neck was scratched up. He also had a long scratch on his back end. This poor goat—he had really been through it. This goat was extremely lucky to be alive. None of his injuries seemed to bother him, and I knew he had been treated medically. All the injuries looked to be healing. His left ear was the worst. He had a really hard scab over and around the ear canal. He did not seem to have any difficulty hearing. I will say, the scab looked fresh. I think the goats had been so interested in Carlos that his ear got hit and the old scab had fallen off. This actually went on for a month. He finally did heal all up and looked great.

I have to say, Carlos has turned out to be the sweetest goat. Things all settled down after a while, and the other goats and donkey were all friends. Lucky and Carlos bonded quickly. They run around the pen together all the time. Carlos loves attention just like the rest of them. He runs to me or Ronnie and wants to be petted. He loves sunflower seeds, animal crackers, and peanuts. He will eat out of my hand without any trouble. He bleats constantly when anyone is outside. He has fit in wonderfully here. The other animals have taken to him really well, surprisingly, and he is now one of them. Even Cracker Jack likes him, and that is saying something. Hercules is hard to handle, and Cracker Jack does not like Hercules. Hercules was the last hold out on accepting Carlos, but he finally did after some time.

I am still in contact with the previous owner of Carlos. He really was a much-loved goat by them. They really did want the best for him. The fears they had about another attack were correct. The lady told me her neighbors had some animals killed by the bobcat as well not long after Carlos was here at the farm. I am happy that he came here. His loving personality fits in well. He is even not opposed to taking selfies with me when he sticks his whole head through the fence. He does this very easily since is missing an ear.

I am going to point out here that it does not matter what you look like or what kind of handicap you may have, it is all about what is in your heart. This goat had a lot of healing to do. He was scared and lucky to be alive. None of that mattered, he is still the sweetest little thing. He is a beautiful goat to me, and his personality makes him even more so. Never let anyone make you feel less that you are because of what you look like. Humans do not build each other up like these animals seem to be doing.

For you created my inmost being; you knit me together in my mother's womb. I praise you because I am fearfully and wonderfully made; your works are wonderful, I know that full well.
—Psalm 139:13–14 (NIV)

CHAPTER 30

Protection

But the Lord is faithful, and he will strengthen
you and protect you from the evil one.
—2 Thessalonians 3:3 (NIV)

Once Carlos came to live here, I noticed something amazing about the animals on the farm. I had not really seen it before, but looking back, it had happened previously. The night Carlos came to live here was when I noticed it, and it continued to this day.

Cracker Jack is a protector by nature. Protection is what a donkey does. As they all went into the shelter, Carlos was in the back corner. When I looked closer, all the other goats were surrounding him in a protective manner, and Cracker Jack stood in front of all them. To me, someone who had not been around farm animals much, this was amazing to see.

Animals are so amazing with their ability to sense things about us. They have emotions and compassion I never knew of a farm animal having these things. They all know when someone is feeling sad or depressed. These animals know when someone has a disability. They know when someone is needing more attention. They also know where the treats are that they are usually so interested in.

I pointed all this out to tell you this story. I am telling this story because I find it important to show how awesome farm animals are. I have a nephew that has Down syndrome. That does not matter to any of us. That kid amazes me. He was here not long ago and wanted to go in the pen with the donkey and goats. I let him in the pen, but I went in also to make sure Hercules did not jump on him. I did not want him to get hurt. Not sure why I thought he would get hurt, that kid was something else.

Hercules amazed me that day. He did not jump on my nephew at all. He did, however, jump on everyone else that went in the pen, including me. Cracker Jack did not try to run him over which he loved to do to most people when he was wanting that attention. Cracker Jack did not want attention; he demanded that attention. Hercules did follow my nephew around the pen the whole time he was out there, except when he was untying other people's shoes. Carlos let him pet on him. I was truly at a loss for words about this. I knew animals were wonderful and smart, but they were so much more than I ever knew was possible. It must be that sixth sense people talk about.

I have also noticed the top hogs in the pigpens are usually the ones that come out of the shelters first to see what is going on. They protect the other pigs, except when they are not trying to steal food from them. Gus does not get far from Treat and Spam even when he is out of the pen on a leash. I see the protective nature they have for each other. Even the ones that do not get along so well have that protectiveness in them. I never knew until I saw it with my own two eyes.

Cracker Jack has always been a great protector. His previous owner had goats and chickens with him at some point, but none of them were ever killed while Cracker Jack was there. I worry about coyotes here because I can hear them close all through the winter months, but all my animals have been good in that there have been no coyote attacks. I think part of it could be Cracker Jack, but most of it is because I pray every night for protection for all my animals. God has protected them all, and I am beyond grateful that prayer works.

I thought the animals protecting one another was important to know. I have never witnessed these things. It does make me wonder why humans cannot do the same thing for each other. The human race could definitely take lessons from farm animals.

CHAPTER 31

Oh, My Sister

Love one another with brotherly affection.
Outdo one another is showing honor.
—Romans 12:10 (ESV)

So before this farm started, probably a year and a half before the farm, my sister wanted us to get animals. She would send me pictures of animals needing homes, and I would say no, we were not ready. She wanted animals here so badly. I kept putting it off. I did not have time to mess with them. We had not checked on the fencing, and we were not ready.

When I finally decided to get animals, she was having to watch them on social media and my blog. She had moved to Canada about six months before we got Cracker Jack. It was hard on me for a bit because she was not here to see me in all these funny stories. In me getting all these animals and most of them all at once really had a huge learning curve for me. I knew she would be here laughing at me. I knew she would be here laughing at me or with me if she could be.

My sister Lacey, her husband Tyler, and their son Tanner were all able to come down for a visit four months after we started the farm. I was so excited for her to see all the animals. She loved animals as much as I did. Most of the family came down for a full day of farm fun when Lacey and her family were in town. We had a house full. Ronnie was home. Lacey, Tyler, Tanner, my mom, my dad, and my grandparents were all here.

I want to tell you the day came with lots of fun with the animals. Cracker Jack tried to knock Lacey over. Hercules untied my grandmother's shoe through the fence. Tanner got to run around the pen with the goats. Tyler was able to get in the pen and meet the animals also. Tanner loved the pigs. He was able to pet Gus while he was out of the pen and walk him on a leash. He threw Cheerios to the big pigs and the little pigs. He really had a good time with the animals. I was excited they all got to meet the animals.

For some reason, it was important to me for my little sister to see I had not forgotten about getting animals and I was not ignoring her when she would send me pictures of animals. She even sent me the best gift for Christmas. It was a book about using animals to help with trauma, which was a dream of mine. It was an amazing gift. I have not had time to read it, but I am looking forward to reading it soon.

I have plans for this sister of mine when she comes back if she does come back to this area. She and I are so much alike with our love for animals. At one point, we lived together when we were both going through a rough time, and we had a zoo in the house. It was quite the time in our lives. We had six dogs, two cats, four frogs, a fish, and a rat. There was an animal we both loved very much until the day he passed away from old age. I am thrilled for what the future holds with the animals and what we can do to help other people through the animals.

CHAPTER 32

What I Have Learned on This Journey

Enter through the narrow gate. For wide is the gate and broad is the road that leads to destruction, and many enter through it. But small is the gate and narrow the road that leads to life and only a few find it.
—Matthew 7:13–14 (NIV)

The most important thing I have learned here is that life will take you on some strange paths to get where you are supposed to be. If someone has told me this is where I would be, I think I would have laughed. However, this life my husband and I have made together is like a dream come true. I put off getting animals because I was not

118

sure how I would do with farm animals. I did not know I would, but I am loving every minute of it. It is hard work but so worth it.

I have learned farm animals are so very emotional, compassionate, and stubborn. They will read your emotions, and they will play on that, good or bad, just like children. I have spoiled them so badly, and they know it.

I have learned that animals love you no matter what. They have that unconditional love and loyalty if you treat them right. The animals can heal your pain if you have any. I know it is not really the animals, but God uses them to show you unconditional love and that can heal whatever pain you might not even know you have. They are good for trauma victims from what I have seen.

I have learned I am stronger than I thought I was. I was able to deal with sick animals, animals running away, animals getting upset with me, and many other things. I had no idea I could deal with these things. Now I do panic, and my husband usually has to talk me down. After he talks me down, I am okay.

I have learned that being outside with the animals every day can cause some problems, especially if the animals are sick or something like that. I have had to endure mange, ringworm, spider bite that turned into cellulitis also, sunburns, mosquito bites, tick bites, etc. I did have all these things in the first year of having animals. I have definitely learned my lesson in these things, and I am more careful so these issues do not get repeated.

I have also learned that if you do not get pigs fixed, they become aggressive. That goes for the males and the females. I did get attacked by one of the females; Bacon Bit was the one that attacked me. I know she did not do it to be mean. She did it because she was in heat. I really did not realize they would attack, but they do. She was sorry afterward and would let me pet her and talk to her. It was like she was apologizing to me for attacking me. The poor girl was having a bad time. She only did that one time. She has not done that since then. I had to realize it was not a malicious attack. The older they get, the worse it can get. This is on my to-do list for sure.

I have learned that rescuing animals is so rewarding. Most of them have lost hope, and seeing them regain that hope is the best thing. I knew this from rescuing my dogs and cats but did not know farm animals would be the same thing, some even more so than a dog or a cat. It is a great feeling doing something for an animal. They can be helpless without someone looking out for them. Farm animals can adapt, but they need people also. This is definitely not an easy job but very rewarding for me.

I have learned I am capable of working hard for these animals. I have been getting up early to feed and water, and I do not like mornings. I have carried buckets of water in the heat. I did not know I was capable of things like that. I knew I could do it I had just never attempted to do it. I can even move railroad ties by myself if I put my mind to it. For me, that is progress within myself. I needed to see these things within myself. God knew I needed to see this for me to continue down the path he is leading me down right not.

I have learned so much about each animal on the farm. Donkeys really are stubborn like I had heard and have said several times in this book. Goats are hilarious with running around the pen and climbing on things. Pigs are the most emotional animal I have ever come into contact with. They love with every bit of their being, unless they are mad and then steer clear of them until they are over it.

I have learned so much with my experience on this small hobby farm we have here. I have learned a lot about myself and about farm animals I did not know. I never knew how wonderful this last year was going to be.

CHAPTER 33

Education

Now these things happened to them as an example,
but they were written down for our instruction,
on whom the end of the ages has come.
—1 Corinthians 10:11 (ESV)

As you have seen and I am sure have at least chuckled about is the lack of knowledge I have had with trying to learn the ends and outs of this farm life. I know some of what I have said really sounded like I did not know what I was doing. This is because I really did not know. I am learning every day. Literally, something new comes up every day.

I want to be absolutely clear in this chapter. I knew nothing about farm animals when we started this. It has had its ups and downs throughout the first year. We are on our second year now, and things are going a little bit smoother. I do not recommend learning as you go. It really makes it harder. I am adding this chapter to give a little bit of information about these animals if you decide you want to get one. It is not easy. These are things I have learned that I did not know but needed to learn for the happiness of the animals. All I wanted for them with each of them coming to this farm is to know love and to have the best life they could here. That is why I rescue these animals.

This I did know but had no idea the extent of it until I rescued pigs. They are not like a dog or a cat. Pigs can take months to a year to bond to their owner. There has to be so much time, love, patience, and understanding that go into a pig trusting a human. It is important to know this going into bringing a pig into your family. It is a commitment to bring any animal into your home.

I was completely oblivious to this when I first got pigs. The potbelly pig population is out of control, just like dogs and cats. It is so bad these potbelly pigs are ending up in the humane societies and the humane societies do what they can, but pigs are not what they usually do. They do not have the correct food or bedding for them. I had no idea about this at all.

What is happening with the population of pigs is this: pigs become mature at a very young age, three to four months old. Pigs are only pregnant three months, three weeks, and three days, so they can have a litter of piglet three times a year. Each litter usually has six to twelve babies. I have heard of litters up to sixteen recently. Even when the boys are neutered, they are not completely sterile for a couple of weeks. It is important to spay and neuter them. It takes away a lot of worry and health problems.

On another note, there is a misconception that potbelly pigs are a "mini" pig. Yes, they are mini if you compare them to a regular size of a farm pig. What is happening is people get these cute little pigs thinking they are going to stay small. When they do not stay small, the owners rehome them. There are not enough homes for these pigs. Across the United States, there are sanctuaries and rescues for these pigs, but they are all full. These poor babies are ending up abandoned on the side of the road. It is awful. It is so sad to me these animals do not have anywhere to go.

Pigs have great memories, and they remember people and what they have been through. They are extremely emotional animals. I had never wanted a pig, so I was clueless with any of this. My stepdaughter had always loved pigs and wanted one so badly. She still does, but she does not have one yet. She gets to come and visit these here on the farm. The pigs can read your emotions. I am astonished by how emotional they are. How wonderful these creatures are.

Pigs need their hooves trimmed. They get vaccinations like cats and dogs. They can be house pig and will use a litter box. They sleep about nine to ten hours in a twenty-four-hour period. They grind their teeth for multiple reasons. They love attention. They can learn all kinds of tricks. They should never eat table scraps. They all get tusks, male tusks have to be cut down. They grow for five years. They act like toddlers. They can live up to twenty years. They shed all their hair in the summer. They get ringworms. They can get ticks on them. Mosquitos can bite them. They throw fits. They can be destructive. Females are aggressive when in heat, males stink so bad when not neutered they usually love to be in the water. They use mud for keeping cool. They do not sweat. They can get sick from stress, and they like blowing bubbles in the water.

An interesting fact that I learned while going through this is, pigs do not show weakness of illness until it is almost too late. If a pig starts to show a sign of illness, they need a vet as soon as possible. Pigs do this because they are a prey animal. They get killed in the wild when they show weakness.

Another interesting thing I have learned is, pigs do not like to be picked up. When they get picked up, they think they are being attacked. That is how it goes in the wild. So when you have a pig and pick it up, you might go deaf in one ear from the screaming. They have a big set of lungs on them and a very high pitch scream. I did not know this when I first got pigs. I knew Spam and Treat screamed, but I was not sure why they were screaming. I picked up Bacon Bit and Pork Chop when they were young thinking that would socialize them quicker, but it did the opposite.

Pigs need a lot of mental stimulation. They get bored easily, so if they are in the house, they will be destructive. Toys are really good for them. They need it to not be bored. This is another reason people rehome their pigs. Pigs become destructive, but what the owner does not realize is the animal is being destructive because they are bored.

Pigs need grass to help with digestion. They love to graze in the grass. They also like to eat hay. Mine go crazy for it and fight over it. On the food issue with pigs, corn is not good for them. It makes them gain weight quickly. Making a potbelly pig overweight gives them health problems. These health problems include obesity, arthritis in the joints because of the extra weight, fat blindness, and many more problems. It is not good for them at all, just like with people.

There is a certain kind of food the pigs need to eat to keep them healthy. It is not okay for them to eat table scraps. That can lead to more of the obesity-related problems. They need pig pellets you can get from the feed stores. This gives them the nutrients they need to stay healthy. The pellets do need to be watered down. This prevents constipation and choking. Constipation can be fatal for potbelly pigs. It is important for this not to happen.

They can also have vegetables. Vegetables give them nutrients to their diets also. It is good for them. Fruits have a lot of sugar in it, so it is not good to give them a lot of fruit. I do give mine fruit only on occasions. Pumpkin is good for them. This helps them to not be constipated also. If they start to get constipated, I give mine pumpkin, and that usually helps them. On occasion, I also give them baby food for a change in pace for them. I usually mix pellets in with the baby food. Diet on a potbelly pig is very important for them to live long and healthy lives. For treats, they get Cheerios.

Pigs need friends that speak their own language. They get lonely without having friends, just like a donkey and goats. It is important to their well-being. Just like us humans, we need relationships to help us through life. I guess animals are like that also. Probably goes back to Noah bringing the animals on the ark two by two.

Animals, all animals, like routine, just like most humans. They know when it is time to eat, when it is time to sleep, when it is time for treats, when it is time for attention. That does not change. I can hear Cracker Jack braying before I get up in the morning. He knows it is time for me to go outside and give him hay. The pigs know also. They are lined up waiting for me as I come outside to get food for them. The dogs know also. They are lined up waiting when I get up. When things get messed up and the routines get offtrack, they do not like it. They have a tendency to throw a few fits.

Donkeys have a temper, at least mine does. He is food aggressive and can definitely be a jerk. Donkeys are so stubborn, and they show it. Cracker Jack actually will walk around and turn his back to me when he is mad. He makes sure I know when he is upset.

Goats are actually like leaves, better than the grass. They are foragers. They cannot anything like I have always heard. If they eat too much of things they should not have, it can cause them to be sick. It is called bloat. I have talked about this earlier in the book. Bloat is uncomfortable for them, and they need medicine to get rid of it and can even be fatal for them.

Goats and coccidiosis is an actual thing also. I know I have talked about that before in this book also. Coccidiosis gives them horrible diarrhea, and the entire herd has to be treated also. I had no idea, but I sure do now. Awful does not describe how bad that really was.

Pigs love to be in the sun. They soak it up. If they do not get enough sun or vitamin D, they start to lose their hair around their eyes. However, if they get too much sun, they do get a sunburn which is painful just like it is for humans.

Animals, all mine, like to sleep in the straw. It keeps them warm at night. You do have to change out the straw in the shelters instead of continuing to add straw to what is already there to prevent mold. The pigs will spread it out for hours to get it exactly the way they want it.

Dogs and pigs do not mix. Poor Daisy loved the pigs when they first came to live here. She would sit by their pen and watch them. She has never hurt one of them, and she actually has saved a couple of them, which I am so grateful for. In the big picture of pigs and dogs, pigs will nip at the dog, and the dog will finish the fight by attacking the pig. A lot of the attacks leave the pigs with no ears and in bad shape. I have seen Gus and Spam trying to get to Daisy through the fence. I could see how things could go so wrong. It happens so quickly. I was glad there was a fence in between them. It was a little scary to watch. I have seen photos of dogs attacking pigs, and it is not a pretty sight.

Pigs root in the dirt. They are pigs. That is what they do. It is instinct for them. Luckily, I do not mind stuff getting rooted up in the pens. If you care about your yard, do not get a pig or block off an area for them to root. They root down to the dirt. Some people would say to put a ring in their nose to stop them from rooting. That looks like animal cruelty to me. It is painful for them to eat or anything up against their nose with a ring in it. A pig rooting is a natural instinct, it is not right to take that away from them.

Pigs love the water. They love to get into a small pool to cool off in the summer hear. However, out in the wild, pigs pee and poop in the water to hide the smell to avoid predator. Well, they do this here now in the pools. Those have to be cleaned daily because of this. I have not figured out a way to stop that since it is a natural instinct. I do not think there is a way to stop it. I just deal with that and clean the pools out daily.

Pig poop stinks and has to be picked up. No excuses, it has to be out of the pen. They like to go in one area, so it is not too bad to pick up. Pigs do not like to be around their own waste. I cannot say I blame them. It gets picked up around here.

I do want to say here that some people might get offended by the names we have named some of the pigs. In the pig community, this is seen as disrespect. I did not know this at all when we got our pigs. I know people like to joke about when we are going to get the pigs ready to eat, but potbelly pigs are not the kind of pig you eat. We named them these names because we thought it was funny. A lot of people do not find this funny. I knew nothing about pigs as you can see when we started this farm and had no idea people would even care what we named them. I did not see anything offensive about it, but I do apologize if someone gets offended by this. When I figured that out, it was already too late. They all knew their names, and I could not change them.

CHAPTER 34

Rescue

And he said to them, "Which of you, having a son
or an ox that has fallen into a well on a Sabbath
day, will not immediately pull him out?"

—Luke 14:5

I would like to talk about the mini pig myth and what is happening to these pigs. I know I have touched on it throughout the book. I know I have mentioned the breeding issues. Here are a few things I have not mentioned.

Pigs are being bred too young to keep the babies small. The momma pigs are being starved when pregnant to keep the babies small. That breaks my heart so much. The babies usually end up having stunted growth, but they also end up with a lot of health issues. I have a pig with some of these issues. I constantly pray over that little thing. Patsy has never looked healthy. She has grown some, but she is still small for her age. She is slow with thought processes also, but I love her. It just takes her more time for things than the other pigs. She is not going anywhere. I will not rehome her because she is a little slow. That gives her more character.

Another thing, some breeders will take the babies from their mom too early and sell them to make them seem like they will stay small. I am not talking about all breeders, but I know several people this has happened to. Like I have said before, when the pigs get bigger than what the breeder had said, the pigs get rehomed. The problem is, there are no homes for these pigs.

The pigs will also get rehomed because of behavioral issues. They have behavioral problems if they are bored. They also have behavioral problems if they have not been spayed or neutered. The females go into heat every twenty-one days. It is important for their health to get them spayed or neutered also. The females get uterine tumors if you do not get them fixed. Males have a horrible smell if they are not fixed. The males and females will both become aggressive when not fixed. There are a lot of accidental pregnancy with pigs when they do not get fixed early. They need to get fixed early also because pigs do not do well under anesthesia after a certain age. It gets dangerous the older they get.

Okay, I will get off that soapbox. I am passionate about this, and I felt it was important to tell you what I have learned while doing research. The last thing I want to say is that if you do decide you want a pig, please adopt one. The sanctuaries and rescues are full, and all those pigs deserve to have homes with a family that will love them. These sanctuaries and rescues do love and care for these animals greatly, but to have them in a home would be fantastic. To adopt a pig, it is more expensive to do so, but they have already been fixed and had their vaccinations. They have also already been socialized, so you would not have to go through some of what I went through. It is a win-win situation. They are the most loving and emotional animals.

Pigs can be the best pet you have ever had if you have the patience for them. They grow for up to five years, so they will be bigger than anticipated. They can live for up to twenty years. They are like toddlers for the entire time they are alive. They beg for attention and scream for food. They throw fits like nothing I have ever seen.

If you would like to adopt a pig, I would be more than happy to help you find one. My goal is to help animals find homes. My dream is to incorporate animals with trauma to teenagers with trauma, let them help each other through life. They need a second chance at life sometimes, and I want to help in that.

CHAPTER 35

Animal Therapy

Do not be anxious about anything, but in every situation, by prayer and petition, with thanksgiving, present your requests to God. And the peace of God, which transcends all understanding, will guard your hearts and your minds in Christ Jesus.
—Philippians 4:6–7 (NIV)

My life was so crazy right during the time we started getting animals. I truly had been running from God for years, and when tragedy struck close to home, I had some decisions to make. I needed to do what I felt God was calling me to do. It was time to turn my life around. I knew if I did not do it then, I might never do it. I will say this: I was not doing anything bad, I just knew I was not doing what God wanted me to do.

I had been doing physical therapy for thirteen years. I was in a job that I really did not like. I knew it was not what I really needed to do with my life. It is a fantastic profession, and some days, I do miss it, but I was not fulfilled by it. I came up with a plan with my husband. Plans do change, though.

My plan was to help teenagers in foster care who have dealt with trauma or drug abuse with animals incorporated with their healing process. That is the reason we started bringing animals home in the first place. I wanted to start a 501(c)(3), possibly a foster home for teenagers and specialize in trauma. I started back to school thinking this would help me in my plans. This had been a dream of mine for years, I just did not want to have to do homework and stuff now that I had a career. I had a name picked out and a mission statement written up and was working on a business plan. I was well on my way. I was doing all the research I could do for this, but plans did change.

I went to a nonprofit close to the town I lived in. The woman who ran the place was someone I had known for twenty years since my troubled teen years. I went by there to take some things to them. I had no idea what was about to happen. I had been shopping, and I kept hearing, "You need to go by there right now." I went in and asked her to hire me. That was not really a plan I had in my head, it just came out. Well, she hired me. They were having a meeting with the foster care system in a few weeks. I just knew this was an answer to prayer. I went to my current job that day and put in my notice. That felt good.

I had no idea how hard this job was going to be on me. The sadness and despair I would see every day was something I had not considered and was not prepared for. To say that was tough on me is an understatement. The job was also bringing back up some trauma I had when I was a teenager that I had no idea was still an issue. This was really tough. It did not sway the thought that I was where I needed to be.

The animals and prayer are the only things that were keeping me going. When I would come home after a particularly rough day, I would go out to feed and water the animals. This always takes most of the evening because I give fresh water and feed them and then have to give each one attention until it was dark outside. When it was a bad day, the animals could tell from my mood. Gus especially would pay me more attention. He was my only friendly one at the time. I would sit down, and he would crawl in my lap and snore. He was saying, "I am here for you." Cracker Jack would try to know me over on those bad days just for me to stop and give him some love. This would make me laugh. Hercules and Romeo would be so needy that I knew they were feeling the pain I was in.

All these animals give me compassion and love on a daily basis, and I do the same for them. They have that unconditional love in them for me. God has a higher love than that for me, so I can only imagine how he feels when one of us is in pain. The animals show me this love every single day, good day or a bad day. God put these animals in my life for a reason. That was to bring me closer to him. He shows his love to me through these animals. I needed these animals as much (or more) than they needed me. I hate that it came through the loss and tragedy of someone special to me and his family, but it gave me the push I needed to see what I was missing. This whole story is because of what I have said in this chapter.

I will say here that I have brought several girls to my house from the nonprofit where I work which is actually a home for young girls who are troubled or pregnant. I am seeing that it is true how animals can help when trauma is involved. They have been here to just see the animals and pet them and love on them. They have been here to swim and eat and just relax in the country. They have been here to work on the farm with all those not-so-fun jobs that have to be done, like adding straw in the pens or working to get the water out of the pen after a big rainstorm. They have been here to pick up poop from the pens. The girls have come by to just watch movies when it is a nasty day outside. They have been here to work on the garden with me. In these days, it is not just the animal that gets to have a good day. The girls become tired and do not have any energy for back talking or getting in trouble. They also can see that whatever they are doing here is helping the animals. Deep down, though, I see the light in their eyes that was dim when getting here and the spar-kly when they leave. Animals just help so much. If nothing else, at least they were able to forget about whatever problems they had since there was work to be done. They do a lot of laughing when they are here at something silly one of them has done or one of the animals has done. The animals know the ones that are hurting the worst, and they usually gravitate toward them. I think this shows so much for me that animals are needed to help with trauma. The love that is seen in these moments, I know this is what I need to be doing. God knows what his plan is in this, and I want to see where it goes. This shows them a love that they never knew with an animal. Some of the girls are scared at first, but they usually get over that, and they just enjoy feeding them or brushing them or just petting them. With the garden, they get to see how things start to grow and how they had a hand in helping the garden grow. I want them to see that life is full of hard work and hard choices, but with God, they can get through it.

If you take away nothing else from this book, know that no matter where you are, God is still with you. I am not a stranger to running away or to not wanting to live the life God put me on this earth for. I have been through pain, trauma, and suffering, but God has pulled me through all that. I may not have seen it then, but I do now. It is never too late to turn back to God. There is no sin too great for God to forgive you. He is still in the same place you left him, so do not give up. If you are struggling with addiction or something else, get help. Reach out to those that love you.

John 3:16 says, "For God so loved the world that He gave His only Son that whoever believes in Him should not perish but have eternal life." It says in 1 Corinthians 10:13–14, "No temptation has overtaken you except what is common to mankind. And God is faithful; he will not let you be tempted beyond what you can bear.

But when you are tempted, he will also provide a way out so that you can endure it." These verses have helped me through some rough times. If you need help, please get it. Someone is waiting to help you. God is listening to your prayers. Do not give up.

Thank you for reading. I hope you enjoyed it. In this second year of rescuing animals, there are actually four more rescues that have taken place here. I hope I can share those stories with you at some point as well. God bless you.

A NOTE FROM SHANNA'S HUSBAND

Shanna is one of the most remarkable people I have ever met. Her heart is drawn to anything—human or animal—that has been stepped on, discarded, mistreated, or abandoned. She started her farm because a donkey was lonely and needed a home. Naturally, the donkey needed friends, so we found three goats. When Shanna and her husband went to pick up the goats, she fell in love with two pot-bellied piglets. Shanna asked her husband, Ronnie, if she could have them. Well, Ronnie thought he was being smart and said, "If you can catch them, you can have them." Next thing you know, Shanna is taking home three goats and two piglets. Shanna loves all her rescues and will tell you, "Everything needs a forever home." You see, if Shanna makes a place in her heart and decides to add you to her flock, herd, or whatever she decides to call it, whatever or whoever she rescues will be shown more love than they have ever known. I speak from firsthand experience. You see, I am her husband, and she rescued me.

Ronnie Kelley

ABOUT THE AUTHOR

Shanna Kelley is a city girl who has gone farm girl and is loving every minute of it. She resides in a small town in Arkansas with her husband and her farm. She has grown children who have lives of their own but do come to visit when they can. She did physical therapy as a physical therapy assistant for thirteen years and decided to quit and go to work in a nonprofit for young girls and women needing some extra help for a short time in their lives. She has just completed her bachelor's degree in psychology and has now written a book. Her hobbies are reading, writing, and quilting. Shanna has a huge heart for animals, and animals have become her passion. She is loving her quiet farm life and wants to share her experiences with you.

CPSIA information can be obtained
at www.ICGtesting.com
Printed in the USA
FSHW020245120221
78470FS